Dis⟨

All quotes, unless otherwise noted, are from the New King James Version. Copyright 1979, 1980, 1982 by Thomas Nelson, Inc. Used by permission. All rights reserved.

Scriptures marked NIV are taken from The Holy Bible, New International Version. Copyright © 1973, 1978, 1984 by International Bible Society. Used by permission of Zondervan Publishing House. All rights reserved.

Scriptures marked KJV are taken from The Holy Bible, King James Version. Copyright © 1972 by Thomas Nelson Inc., Camden, New Jersey 08103.

Scriptures marked NLT are taken from The Holy Bible, New Living Translation. Copyright © 1996, 2004, 2007 by Tyndale House Foundation. Used by permission of Tyndale House Publishers, Inc., Carol Stream, Illinois 60188. All rights reserved.

Noah

Surviving the Storm

Richard Holmes

Copyright: 2014 Richard Holmes
ISBN: 978-1-61194-991-9
All rights reserved.

Distributed by Belle Compass Books

Cover Design: Debra Dixon
Ark (manipulated) © Javier Cruz Acosta | Dreamstime.com

Dedication

To my wife, MaLeah. It's because of your unending encouragement and support that this dream came true. Thank you!

Table of Contents

Introduction

There's no doubt that we live in a dark world. We need look no further than recent school and church shootings or mass shootings, like the ones in Las Vegas and Florida, to see evidence of this darkness. These actions certainly exemplify the evil in the world, but actions aren't the only way to reveal the malevolence of the world—our very thoughts do as well. Our generation isn't the only one that's faced this kind of spiritual oppression. In Noah's days, the world was so dark that God chose to destroy it and start over with Noah's family. God called Noah to be the light in his generation. And God is calling you to be a light in yours.

God placed a huge calling on Noah's life. His family would build something that had never been built (or even contemplated, for that matter). They would weather the storm that destroyed the rest of the world because of their obedience, and then they would repopulate the earth. But, they weren't perfect—just like you're not perfect. God knew they weren't perfect. Before God ever called Noah, He knew Noah would mess up. The best part is that didn't stop Him. You can't disqualify yourself from God's plans with your own faults and weaknesses.

If knowing that Noah would mess up didn't stop God from placing a massive calling on his life, knowing that you'll mess up won't stop God from placing a massive calling on *your* life. Will you believe the lies of the enemy that you can't—that you're not enough—or will you heed the call of God?

We all have storms in our lives. We all have trials. But, we also have all we need to make it to the other side of the storm, because God has given it to us. If we listen to Him and follow His lead, we'll come out the other side better than ever. It's up to you, though. You choose who to listen to and who to follow.

Follow me on this journey with Noah. We'll see how God called Noah to be a light for his generation. We'll explore Noah's call to build and how Noah was obedient even though it didn't make much sense at the time. We'll talk about all the hard work that goes into answering God's call and how He knows exactly what we need to make it through the storm on the horizon. Then, we'll see Noah leave the ark that he and his family had worked hard over the span of decades to build. We'll explore the difficulty we often experience when it's time for us to leave one season of our lives and head into the next. Finally, we'll see what happens once the storm is over.

We can all be encouraged by Noah and his obedience. We aren't perfect, just like Noah wasn't perfect. But, just like God used an imperfect person like Noah to shape the world, He can use an imperfect person like you to shape the world. Whether you let Him is completely up to you.

Chapter 1

Light in the Darkness

A Man Named Noah

And he called his name Noah, saying, "This one will comfort us concerning our work and the toil of our hands, because of the ground which the Lord has cursed." (Genesis 5:29)

Do you ever feel like things can't keep going the way they are—that something has to change? I know I have. When I look at the world around me, I often have those thoughts. And they're nothing new. Actually, that line of thinking has been around for millennia.

That's exactly how a man named Lamech felt thousands of years ago. As he looked at his culture's trajectory, Lamech understood things couldn't keep going the way they were. Something *had* to change. You may assume that Lamech lived in Sodom or Babylon—cities we often associate with the very height of carnality. But he didn't. Lamech lived in a far more troubling world—one in which peoples' very thoughts were totally evil. Surveying the condition of the earth and its inhabitants, Lamech had to wonder if he and his wife had made the right decision to bring a child into the world. But, the decision had been made and Lamech's wife was about to give birth to their son.

Lamech knew not only that things *needed* to change, but also that they were *going* to change. He sensed something was different about his baby boy—he wasn't going to be like everyone else. Lamech felt his new son's life had an assignment and a purpose. In fact, he knew his son was going to be instrumental in bringing about the necessary change. That's why Lamech named his son Noah, which means "rest, relief, or comfort." In Genesis 5:29, Lamech prophesied about Noah, saying, "[t]his one will comfort us concerning our work and the toil of our hands, because of the ground which the Lord has cursed." He couldn't have imagined just how accurate both his discernment and prophecy would be when they unfolded some six-hundred years later.

Noah's generation was far worse than the sexual sin of Sodom or the debauchery of Babylon. Obviously, God took Sodom and Babylon seriously (to the point of destroying both cities due to their evil actions). But, they still weren't as detrimental as the culture in Noah's generation. Things in Noah's day were so off course, so evil, that—for the only time in history—God destroyed the *entire world*.

Genesis 6:5 describes Noah's generation. The scripture doesn't focus on the people's *actions*, but, rather, on their *thoughts*. *The LORD observed the extent of human wickedness on the earth, and He saw that everything they thought or imagined was consistently and totally evil.* (Genesis 6:5 NLT)
Think about that: the only time we see God's anger poured out in such an explosive and demonstrative way, it was not due to what people *did*. It was due to what they *thought*. Your thought life matters.

Actions caused the destruction of a city, but thoughts caused the destruction of the world.

> *And the Lord said, "My Spirit shall not strive with man forever, for he is indeed flesh; yet his days shall be one hundred and twenty years." (Genesis 6:3)*

Light in the Darkness

> *Then the Lord saw that the wickedness of man was great in the earth, and that every intent of the thoughts of his heart was only evil continually. And the Lord was sorry that He had made man on the earth, and He was grieved in His heart. So the Lord said, "I will destroy man whom I have created from the face of the earth, both man and beast, creeping thing and birds of the air, for I am*

sorry that I have made them."
(Genesis 6:5-7)

We tend to concern ourselves with others' actions. We become so wrapped up in what's going on around us that we lose track of our surroundings. I remember my dad taking me to the neighborhood park to play when I was around eight or nine years old. I climbed the ladder of the slide, but, as I approached the top step, I got distracted watching some of the other kids playing on the see-saw and swings. As I continued to watch them play, I stepped onto the top step of the slide's ladder. I was ready to slide to the bottom—only I didn't. Instead, I had become so wrapped up in what others around me were doing that I stepped the wrong way off the top of the slide and fell to the ground. Boy did I hit hard. It knocked the wind right out of me. I learned a valuable and painful lesson that day: Don't get distracted by the actions of others; instead, keep looking ahead and focus on your next step. Otherwise, your next step may lead you into easily-avoided pain.

While our culture obsesses about people's actions (just like I did that day at the playground), God is more interested in people's thoughts. That's His focus in Genesis 6:5-7. But, why? It's because every action *begins* with a thought. Thoughts are like seeds. When allowed to germinate, these seeds grow into the fruit of action. God is not as concerned with the fruit as He is with the seed from which it grows. Bad seeds cause problems with our thoughts—problems that, when we act on them, eventually produce bad fruit. Simply put, bad thoughts lead to bad actions.

If a tree produces bad fruit, you have a couple choices. You could just cut away the limbs where the bad fruit grows and toss them aside. And, that may even work for a while—but covering up the symptoms will never produce permanent change. Eventually, the other limbs will start bearing that same bad fruit. The other option is to look to the real problem: the issue with the seed. It's the same for us. When our actions are bad, we have those same choices. We can try to change our actions—and, like the tree, things may improve for a little while. But, if we want real, lasting change, we have to repair our thoughts. It all begins in our minds.

That's why Satan focuses so much of his attention on our thoughts. I have a flash drive on my keychain. You probably have one somewhere, too. When I want to use a file from my laptop on another computer, I just copy the master onto the flash drive. When I do that, the information on the copy is a duplicate of the original. That's what Satan wants to do with our thoughts. He wants to copy his thoughts and paste them into our minds. Satan wants his thoughts to become your thoughts and his way of thinking to become your way of thinking.

You may be thinking, "how does that happen? How does the enemy make me think like him?" It's simple. Satan uses the power of suggestion to set up strongholds in your mind. He suggests things to you all day, every day. When a suggestion comes, you have to decide what to do with it: you can agree with it or you can arrest it. Ultimately, you are the decider. Here's the thing, though—his suggestions are powerless unless you agree with them. If you don't agree to meditate on these thoughts, you aren't thinking like the enemy, and you've kept him from setting up his stronghold inside your mind.

The enemy's suggestions may start out small—as some-thing that seems insignificant at the time. Perhaps it's a sugges-tion that you just don't have time to pray or get into the Word today. The suggestion is that you can jump right back into your routine tomorrow. Only tomorrow passes and that same suggestion wins again. Then it's a week and you haven't picked up your Bible or talked to your Father. At first, you may have known the suggestion wasn't quite right, that it's out of character for you, or even totally out of line with God's Word. But, once you agreed with the suggestion, then you tried to find a way to justify it. In an attempt at justification, you may have thought things like, "that's right—I *don't* have time to get in the Word. I'm exhausted. I've been working hard. I've been going through a lot. I've been really stressed out."

When you try to justify the enemy's suggestion, you meditate on it. Do you think you don't know how to meditate? Let me assure you: if you know how to worry, you know how to meditate. Once you've mediated on the suggestion and justified it, you're well on the way to allowing Satan to copy and paste his way of thinking right onto your internal flash drive—as easy as clicking a mouse. Eventually, the enemy's suggestion plants a seed that turns into a way of thinking. The thoughts produced by the seed turn into the fruit of wrong actions. All of this from one little suggestion—something you likely realized wasn't quite right from the start.

See how easy it was? The enemy produced the suggestion: a thought. You dwelled and meditated on it. Then, before you knew it, the bad seed turned into bad fruit. You gave the thought legs and it became action. Are you starting to get it? Your thoughts are the genesis for all your actions.

But, remember, you still have a choice. You can choose to arrest the enemy's suggestion rather than accepting it. How do you do that? You have to fight with the right weapons. Like every other area of life, God's Word tells you exactly what you need to do. 2 Corinthians 10:4-5 (NIV) says: "The weapons we fight with are not the weapons of the world. On the contrary, they have divine power to demolish strongholds. We demolish arguments and every pretension that sets itself up against the knowledge of God, and we take captive every thought to make it obedient to Christ."

That scripture gives us the blueprint: we demolish the enemy's strongholds by making our thoughts line up with God's thoughts rather than with Satan's. You can choose to agree with the enemy's suggestion *or* you can choose to arrest the thought and bring it under obedience. At the end of the day, when a thought doesn't feel right or you know it to be off, ask yourself, does this align with God's Word. If yes, you know it to be encouraging, enriching, or even correcting. If no, release it. Don't let it build a stronghold. If you let it germinate, sooner or later that seed will produce fruit—and you're not going to like the taste of it. You'll think "why did I ever *do* that?" But, your real focus should be on "why did I ever *think* that?"

And God saw that the wickedness of man was great in the earth, and that every imagination of the thoughts of his heart was only evil continually. (Genesis 6:5 KJV)

That's why thoughts are so important—they grow into actions. In the time of Genesis 6, evil thinking and imagination dominated the world. In the original Hebrew, the word imagination means, "what can be formed in the mind." Think about that. *Everything* formed in the minds of men across this entire landscape of humanity in Noah's day was evil. The world was consumed by total darkness. Total darkness that is, except for one solitary ray of light.

Genesis 6:8 tells us, "But Noah found grace in the eyes of the Lord." So, here's this man named Noah, who, in the midst of this great darkness, chose to be different. He stood out as a beacon of light in his generation. One *man*—not an angel, just a normal man—stood out as a leader of hope for the future.

The Light of the World

In Matthew 5:14, Jesus told his followers, "You are the light of the world." Just as in Jesus's time, his followers today still have that calling. In our age of great darkness, *you* are called to be the light of the world. While everyone else gives in to the darkness of their thoughts, God placed you exactly where you are to be the light in that darkness. You weren't born into your family by chance. You don't have your job by accident. You don't live in your neighborhood by coincidence. God ordained and ordered your steps to be placed in the middle of specific darkness. God has not set you up for failure. He has placed you with a purpose.

The same was true for Noah. God placed Noah in that particular generation to be His light. Noah stood alone for God in the darkness that engulfed the world around him. He lived in a time when things were so bad that God said, "I'm sorry I ever made man." Literally *everyone* outside of Noah's family had turned their backs on God. Noah lived for God all by himself.

What an amazing testimony! Noah stayed faithful to the Lord even though he had no local church for support. He didn't have a life group to connect with every week. He didn't have a prayer partner whom he called on when things began to close in around him. He didn't have a praise and worship team to sing that *one* song that would make him feel better when he was discouraged. He didn't have podcasts, The Message on Sirius XM, TBN, DayStar, or Moody radio. Noah didn't even have his favorite worship album on his iTunes account to play so he could feel the presence of God. He only had God. And that will always be enough.

I can't imagine how Noah felt. I know I've had times in my spiritual journey when I felt alone. I started preaching the Gospel at the young age of 14. I can tell you that the public- school system wasn't exactly an encouraging environment for a young minister going through high school. But, no matter how isolated I felt in that setting, I had something Noah didn't: I had the strength of my church family to lean on to help me stay strong through those difficult years. There's a reason why we are told to not forsake the assembling of believers together.

Most of us struggle to stay faithful to God even with an impressive support system at our beck and call. You can get in your car and turn on Christian radio or open up your iTunes library on your phone. You can come to church multiple times a week. We have Christian television. We have the Bible—and we can even have someone else read us the Word of God from our Kindle or smartphone. We have people who will pray for us, life groups for fellowship, and church services for training and equipping us. We have everything in the world to help us; yet, we still struggle.

Then there's Noah. Can you grasp the pressure on him to just give in and be like everybody else?

At work Monday morning his co-workers ask, "Noah, what'd you get into this weekend?"

"Well," he answers, "I went to church."

"Really? So, who was there? Big crowd this week?"

"Just me and my family. How 'bout you? What'd you do?"

"I can't remember, but, man, it was fun. You've gotta come with us next time!"

"No, I need to be in church."

"But Noah, it's been fifty years now. You and your family

12

are *still* the only ones there. It's not grown at all. Give it up! You're all by yourself! Just come party and hang out with us, man. Loosen up. Everybody's doing it. You're lame! Just give it up and come join the crowd."

Can you imagine the pressure he felt every minute of every day to be like everybody else—to give in and quit the "God thing?" Yet, in the face of all that pressure—in the face of that persecution—he continued to live for God. Everyone else was unified in the easier, lower path, but Noah stood tall for God.

Standing for God

Noah wasn't the only person in scripture who stood for God when everyone else around him bowed down. You'll find some of the most powerful examples of this in the Book of Daniel. In the face of the lions' den, the young prophet Daniel said, "I'm still going to pray. I'm still going to talk to God, serve Him, and have a relationship with Him." He stayed strong and didn't bow down to that pressure—not even when it looked as if his very life was on the line. Daniel's friends, Shadrach, Meshack, and Abednego faced a fiery furnace of certain death, but when everyone else bowed down and worshipped a false god, these three continued to stand for the one true God. They stayed strong. (Daniel 1-3 and 6).

There's a verse in the New Testament that's more obscure, but the story it tells is just as powerful. Philippians 4:22 shows us we can stand for God even when everyone else is bending under the weight of other influences. It reads, "All the saints greet you, but especially those who are of Caesar's household." As he penned this letter to the church in Philippi, Paul was in a prison in Rome. Paul sent this letter to encourage the church to be obedient to God. He told the Philippians that all the Christians in Rome say hello, but *especially those in Caesar's household.* The amazing thing here is that there were *any* Christians in Caesar's household. Caesar was the title for the Emperor of Rome, and the particular Caesar Paul wrote about was Nero. To put that into perspective, the first imperially-supported persecution of Christians began under Nero. He sent Christians to die in the

Colosseum for *sport*. If that wasn't bad enough, Nero was also known to have Christians arrested, hanged, and lit on fire to illuminate his gardens by night. That's the guy Paul's talking about.

Yet, Paul says there are Christians living in Nero's house. To put that in today's terms, in our world, people turn away from Jesus because someone took their parking spot, unfriended them on Facebook, or talked about them at the water cooler. As a pastor, I've seen this happen far too many times. Unfortunately, I've seen people walk away from their fellowship with God and God's people for everything ranging from someone not shaking their hand at church to people not complimenting their chicken and dumplings enough at the potluck dinner. Our generation lets the offenses of the world keep us from worshipping Jesus. We let such petty things stand between us and God, but, the saints in Nero's house refused to even let certain death stand in their way. These Christians lived in a house where just speaking the name of Jesus meant death. Some of them might have seen their loved ones thrown to the lions or watched as their bodies burned to cinders in the gardens. But, they still lived for Christ. It was *that* important to them.

If there can be saints in Caesar's household, there can be saints in your household! If there can be people who live for God in the face of certain death, there can be people who live for God right in the comfort of your hometown. Remember, God put you where you are for a reason. Maybe *you're* the person in your workplace or your family whom God placed there to be His light in the darkness. Learn from Noah and Daniel and the Christians in Caesar's household. Their influence didn't feel like it was growing. Noah wasn't reaching new people or growing the church. But that didn't stop any of them from trying. Their fruit was good even though their numbers were bad. Don't let your perceived outcome negate your good seed.

Jesus Is the Light and the Life

Then Jesus spoke to them again, saying, "I am the light of the world. He who follows Me shall not walk in darkness, but have the light of life." (John 8:12)

"In Him was life, and the life was the light of men. And the light shines in the darkness, and the darkness did not comprehend it." (John 1:4-5). The darkness could not put out the light; and, if you're born again, that same light is inside you. No matter how dark the world may be around you, it cannot put out the light of God inside of you. Think about it: if you walk into a room where all the lights are off and you turn on just one single light, the darkness must leave. It has no choice. If that's the case, how much greater is the light of God living inside you than that sixty-watt bulb that made the darkness flee from the room? Darkness may completely surround you; but, I can tell you that the darkness of the world is *not* greater than the light of God inside you. The Holy Spirit led and directed you to the place you're in so the light inside you can conquer the darkness—not for the darkness to conquer you.

You can be pure while everyone else around you is polluted. You can be strong when everyone else around you is weak.

How do I do that?
How can I be pure?
How can I be a light in the darkness?
How can I be Noah in my generation?

Noah was living in a time in which the thoughts of those around him were continually evil. What made him different? Noah was different because his *thoughts* were different. Proverbs 23:7 says, "As [a man] thinks in his heart, so is he." Since you are what you think, different living begins with different thinking.

Don't copy the behavior and customs of this world, but let God transform you into a new person by changing the way you think. Then you will learn to know God's will for you, which is good and pleasing and perfect. (Romans 12:2 NLT)

God's Word is clear: we aren't supposed to be like everyone

else around us who has given in to the darkness. We shouldn't copy the behavior of the world, but, rather, let God transform us by changing how we think. The word "transform" is the Greek word *metamorpho*, meaning "to undergo a metamorphosis." But, how do you do that? You start by the renewing of your mind. Only once you've renewed your mind can you manifest the good, pleasing, and perfect will of God for your life. When you do this, people around you will notice your light. When you do this, the darkness has no choice but to flee.

You change your life when you change your thinking.

You were saved immediately—the very moment you made the choice to accept Jesus as Lord and Savior—but the renewing of your mind is a process. And, it's a choice: you have to *choose* to renew your mind. You have to actively pursue the transformation of your life through the renewal of your mind. And, again, you change your life when you change your thinking.

The problem is that many of us are so focused on changing what we *do*, that we never focus on changing how we *think*. We start off strong, thinking, "I'll stop [fill in the blank: cussing, drinking, lying, etc.]." But, after a few days or a couple of weeks, we end up going back to our old bad actions. The bad decisions keep happening because we're working at the fruit level rather than the seed level. Remember that fruit tree we talked about? You know, the one with the bad fruit. Cutting a limb from that tree didn't stop it from bearing the very same fruit it had born before. In much the same way, when we only try to fix our actions rather than our thoughts, we continue producing bad fruit. We're just trimming limbs.

> *Let this mind be in you which was also in Christ Jesus.*
> (Philippians 2:5)

In the church world, you'll hear ten thousand sermons about living like Jesus. But, what you may not realize is that it's impossible to *live* like Jesus until you first *think* like Him. Just like the wrong thinking of Noah's generation brought about the destruction of the entire world, countless people in our generation destroy their own personal worlds with their thoughts. Conversely, just like wrong thinking can destroy your personal world, right thinking can build it up.

> *Casting down arguments and every high thing that exalts itself against the knowledge of God, bringing every thought into captivity to the obedience of Christ.* (2 Corinthians 10:5)

Noah Thought Differently

> *When the Son of Man returns, it will be like it was in Noah's day. In those days before the flood, the people were enjoying banquets and parties and weddings right up to the time Noah entered his boat. People didn't realize what was going to happen until the flood came and swept them all away. That is the way it will be when the Son of Man comes.* (Matthew 24:37-39 NLT)

Everyone around Noah was just living for the moment, but Noah was thinking about his legacy.

Our current generation shares three distinct thoughts and beliefs with Noah's.

1. Just live for today. There is an anthem that rules this generation: YOLO—You Only Live Once. It's what people say before making a dumb decision or doing something stupid. You scream "YOLO" and get the tattoo you'll regret ten years later. You spend money on something you didn't think through and couldn't afford—money you'll soon wish you had back. The problem is, the phrase is a lie. Eternity is real. You *don't* only live once. In fact, you live forever—either in heaven with Christ or in hell with Satan. Aside from the eternal aspect, the truth is, you'll also live on through your legacy. Your legacy is the fruit of your years and your decisions, and it outlives your last breath. Your legacy and reputation and character will march on long after your walk on earth is done.

Everyone around Noah was just living for the moment, but Noah was thinking about his legacy. If you are going to be the Noah of your generation—the single light that breaks through the darkness—you need to live for more than just today. You need to live with legacy in mind. In the last several years, the body of Christ has exhibited an unhealthy focus, professing the subtle deception that we just need to pray for the rapture. Now, I'll be the first to pray the prayer, "Come quickly, Lord Jesus." But what if Jesus doesn't come tomorrow, next year, ten years from now, or even a hundred years from now? What's your legacy?

Jesus said for us to occupy (meaning "do business") until He returns. But, what kind of business should we do? We should do the same business He told Mary and Joseph He was about when He was twelve years old: "Don't you know I must be about my Father's business?" (Luke 2:49). He never said go huddle up and pray for the rapture. Jesus said go out in the highways and hedges and compel people to come in so that His house may be full. What business are you about?

If you buy into the "only live for today" mentality, that means you see your life as devoid of meaning and purpose. If you believe God has no plan and no assignment for your life, then you can freely live for the moment, because you see no consequences. But, if you really believe there is a purpose for you on this earth, then that purpose guides your decisions and brings boundaries to your life; if you believe you have a purpose, you don't want to do anything in violation of that purpose. But, if the enemy can convince you that you have no purpose, destiny, or assignment, then you believe it really doesn't matter what you do. After all, it couldn't affect your purpose—because you have none.

Simply put, you have to know you have a purpose to be legacy-minded rather than just thinking and living for the moment. Are you a person of purpose?

If you are going to be the Noah of your generation—a light in the darkness—you must allow the Holy Spirit (not pain) to be your teacher.

2. Only change when it hurts badly enough. Genesis 6:39 says, "People didn't realize what was going to happen until the flood came and swept them all away" (NLT).

2 Peter 2:5 says, "[God] did not spare the ancient world, but saved Noah, one of eight people, a preacher of righteousness, bringing in the flood on the world of the ungodly." Noah was preaching righteousness—both as a preacher in the traditional sense and through the boat he built.

Now imagine, this guy is building a large boat over a period of several years. At some point, it's bound to come up in conversation at the community barbeque. Sometime, Noah was going to run into his neighbors at the food exchange, and they were certain to ask him, "Noah, what's up with the boat?"

Noah would have said something like, "Well, I was talking to God one day, and He said it's going to rain. In fact, God said all of creation is going to be destroyed unless we repent. So, He told me to build this boat to save my household. I wanna tell you something: y'all need to repent."

Noah preached through his actions and through his vocation. How you go to work each day preaches. How you relate to your customers preaches. How you relate to your spouse and your children preaches. How you react to your fellow parents and the officials at the ballgame preaches. Preachers get one, maybe two hours with people a week. You live the gospel every minute. Your life preaches. Noah building the ark raised some questions; and he took the opportunity to present the gospel through his answers.

Noah preached, but his generation didn't listen. Well, they probably *listened* in the literal sense of the term, but they didn't *hear* what he said—or, more accurately, they didn't hear for seventy-five years. Then, the rain started falling. One of our common thoughts today is, "if I'm not suffering—if I'm not *really* hurting—then I don't need to change." God speaks to us in lots of ways: through our daily walk with Him, through His Word, through prayer, life groups, and relationships.

God not only speaks to us in a variety of ways, He also speaks to us through a variety of people: our friends, family, pastors, and church family. But what's our response? Typically, when God speaks, we say, "I hear you, God, but I don't really need to change. Life's still pretty good." We do what the people in Noah's day did, and we say, "I'll wait another day."

I've witnessed firsthand the harm this kind of thinking leads to. We think things like: "My wife is still with me. She hasn't left me yet, so it can't be that bad." Or maybe it's, "I'm not addicted. I don't care what anyone says. I've got this under control. I can stop anytime I want." Then, there's, "I still have my house, my family, and my health. It's not that serious." It's hard to sit back and watch as people delay making wise choices until the pain of their immaturity becomes unbearable. But, I've seen it time and time again. For us, it may not be seventy-five years like in Noah's generation. It may be seventy-five hours, days, weeks, or months. However long it takes, the pain will catch up to us. It always does. If you're going to be a light in the darkness, and the Noah in your generation, you can't allow pain to be your teacher. You have to grow to the point where you can see the pain coming and correct yourself before it hurts. Instead of pain, you need to allow the Holy Spirit to teach you.

Jesus said when the Holy Spirit comes, He would guide us into all truth. The problem is, the Church doesn't really like the Holy Spirit teaching us. We'd rather be taught by pain. It's only when everything starts to fall apart that we finally do what God had been telling us we needed to do for the last seventy-five years. That holds just as true today as it did in Noah's time.

3. Look to God for rescue, not relationship. Noah's generation wanted nothing to do with God—that is, until the rain started to fall. Once the storm hit, then they wanted God to rescue them. Does that sound familiar? People don't want to hear about God until the clouds form and the rain starts to fall—only then do they cry out to God. We live apathetically toward God and don't think anything about Him. In fact, our society thinks those who really live close to the Lord are fanatical—or maybe even a little crazy. Then, the clouds start to form, the thunder starts rolling, and the biggest storm we've ever faced is bearing down on the horizon. Only then do we want everybody to pray for us. When our storm begins, we memorize scripture and go to the house of God eight days a week. We call on the name of God and get really close to the Lord.

Then the clouds part, the rain lifts, and the sun starts coming back out. When that happens, we're once again so busy we sleep in on Sunday. We put off Bible study and prayer until we're more refreshed and less pressed for time. Before we know it, a week has turned into a month, one month has turned into six, and we're right back in the same place we were before our storm. In our heart of hearts, God is just a rescuer. We just look to Him when we need rescuing from the storm. That mentality wasn't exclusive to Noah's generation—it's in ours, too.

Noah was a just man, perfect in his generations. Noah walked with God. (Genesis 6:9)

Before there was a flood, Noah walked with God. Before the first cloud formed, Noah walked with God. Before the first drop of rain came, Noah walked with God. Before he ever picked up a hammer, Noah walked with God. Noah walked with God for the sake of relationship—just because he loved God. He *wanted* to walk with God. That's what made the Lord say, "I can trust this man to build something that will change the course of history."

I've come to realize there's nothing in life we can come up against that we can't overcome by just continuing to walk with God. I want you to ask yourself: "Am I walking with God?"

The Light in the Darkness Key Points

Review these key points and begin to renew your thinking as you strive to be a light in the darkness to this generation.

• Actions caused the destruction of a city, but thoughts caused the destruction of the world.

• You change your life when you change your thinking.

• It's impossible to *live* like Jesus until you first *think* like Him.

• Everyone around Noah was just living for the moment, but Noah was thinking about his legacy.

• Have a relationship with God. He is there for relationship, not rescue.

Being a Light in the Darkness Action Steps

Being a light in the darkness of this generation requires action on your part. Read the suggested action steps below and check them off as you complete them. Add your own as the Lord continues to instruct you.

*Make financial and relational decisions with legacy in mind—not just for today.

* If you really believe there is a purpose for you on this earth, then that purpose guides your decisions and brings boundaries to your life. You aren't going to do anything that would violate your purpose. Write out your purpose

_____

* Ask yourself before you make any major decision in life: "How will what I'm considering affect my children and my grandchildren? How will it affect my destiny and purpose?"

* Determine not to allow pain to be your teacher. Instead, invite the Holy Spirit to teach you.

* Determine to be the Noah of your generation and walk with God no matter your situation. Declare: "I've come to realize that there's nothing in life that I can come up against that I can't overcome by just continuing to walk with God."

* What else is God showing you to do to become a light in the darkness to this generation?

At work

_____

At home

In your community

Chapter 2

The Call to Build

Noah Pleases God

This is the genealogy of Noah. Noah was a just man, perfect in his generations. Noah walked with God. And Noah begot three sons: Shem, Ham, and Japheth. The earth also was corrupt before God, and the earth was filled with violence. So God looked upon the earth, and indeed it was corrupt; for all flesh had corrupted their way on the earth. And God said to Noah, "The end of all flesh has come before Me, for the earth is filled with violence through them; and behold, I will destroy them with the earth. Make yourself an ark of gopher wood; make rooms in the ark, and cover it inside and outside with pitch. (Genesis 6:9-14)

These verses describe God calling Noah to begin building the ark. What an amazing and awesome task to begin a construction project that is not only going to change his and his family's life, but is literally going to change the world. Remember that this invitation—this calling to build—didn't come from a construction company; it came directly from God. Noah is not the only person God ever called to build something. God calls *each of us* to build.

The universal call on all our lives is to build God's Kingdom. God's Kingdom is built through people. It's built through relationships. If we don't like people, consistently damage relationships with others, or just don't know how to connect with others, we will be greatly limited in our ability to build God's Kingdom. How we relate with people reflects our hearts. God must work in our hearts so He can use us to build His Kingdom. God first builds His Kingdom *in* us, so He can then build His Kingdom *through* us.

We also each have a specific and individual call to build in our lives. We all have seasons in which God calls us to build different things. God may call you to focus on building your marriage or family for a specific season in your life; God may call you to focus on building an education you can use to build His Kingdom and bring glory to His name in the later part of your life; or God could call you to focus on building your finances, career, or business for a particular season.

> For **God saved us and called us** to live a holy life. He did this, not because we deserved it, but because that was his plan from before the beginning of time—to show us his grace through Christ Jesus. (2 Timothy 1:9 NLT) (emphasis added)

This is very clear and is not something to be taken lightly. It is a holy calling and it is not according to our works, but according to His own purpose and grace. God's calling on your life predates the beginning of the world. Take a minute to let that soak in.

God doesn't build your calling based on your circumstances. He builds your circumstances based on your calling.

God's Calling on Your Life

God allows or orchestrates the circumstances of your life in accordance with His calling on your life. He doesn't build your calling based on your circumstances. He builds your circumstances based on your calling. He has saved you *and* He has called you. You can't have one without the other. You can't say, "I'm saved but I don't think God has a calling on my life." Paul clearly says in 2 Timothy 1:9 that you are **saved and called**. In fact, you were called before you were saved. You were purposed before He formed you in your mother's womb.

God told Jeremiah, "Before I formed you in your mother's

womb I knew you. I purposed you, I designed you, I called you to be a prophet to the nations." (Jeremiah 1:5 author paraphrase). Just like Jeremiah's calling, God had *your* calling set long before your mommy ever knew your daddy. God had your calling set long before the circumstances of your life, your challenges, situations, difficulties, and handicaps ever came about. Because God had your calling in mind, He knew what family, community, generation, time, and skill set you would need to complete it. God looked around and said that time and those people, they're going to need one of you. And He knew you were going to need those challenges and those people. You are saved *and* called.

Because God had your calling in mind, He knew what family, community, generation, time, and skill set you would need to complete it.

There are a few facts we need to understand about the calling God has placed on our individual lives. First off, God may call you to do something that doesn't make sense. God called Noah to build an ark. That didn't make sense! Not only had there never been an ark built before, it had *never even rained*. There had never been a need in the world as Noah knew it for a boat of any size—let alone one of the magnitude God called Noah to build. When Noah received the call of God to build this boat, he didn't reject God's instructions on the grounds that they didn't add up mathematically or that they wouldn't look good on a profit and loss statement.

2 Timothy 1:9 says the call of God for your life is not according to your works, but according to His purpose. It is not according to what we think or according to what makes sense to us. It is according to God's purpose and God's design. Your job is to obey God, step out, and do what God calls you to do. If you wait until it makes sense, you're never going to be living in obedience to God.

God's plan will rarely make sense to the limited mind of man. In fact, the Word of God says that God's thoughts are not our thoughts and God's ways are not our ways. They are higher than ours (Isaiah 55:8) and beyond our ability to conceptualize. The minute we think we have God figured out, we've missed it. He can't be put in our box or explained with our limited vocabulary.

I've personally experienced God calling me to make a move that made no sense at the time. When God began dealing with my wife, MaLeah, and me about pastoring in eastern Kentucky, I wasn't exactly enthused about the prospect. In my pride and ignorance, I envisioned life and ministry in a metropolitan area— or at least in a medium-sized city. When someone would ask, "Where do you sense God leading you?" the hills and hollers of Appalachia weren't on my radar. After months of prayer, conversations with trusted friends, and talking things out with MaLeah (I'll be transparent here: we argued—she knew it was God and I didn't want to admit it), it became clear to me that those ideas were just that—they were my ideas and not God's. So, MaLeah and I moved hours away from family and the life we'd known and relocated to Pikeville, Kentucky. In those lonely and uncertain hours driving a U-Haul truck up US 23, we had no idea what we would face. I called a pastor friend who had been helpful to me as I was getting started in ministry to tell him about our transition. He said, "Why in the world would you want to spend the best years of your life trying to do something there? It doesn't make sense." And, he was right: it didn't make sense. There were no guarantees. The only thing we were certain of was that we *had* to obey God. The blessing on the other side of that obedience has been far greater than anything we could have hoped for. We've seen hundreds of people receive Jesus as their Lord and Savior and grow as followers of Christ. We've seen families changed by the grace of God. What initially looked like a big ball of crazy has unfolded into a beautiful picture of God's sovereignty.

Just like God's plan for my life didn't make any sense to me at the time, remember that God may call *you* to do some things that don't make sense, either. In fact, I would say if you feel like what God is calling you to do doesn't make any sense, it very well could be the *confirmation* that it is from God. As you see through reading the stories, God has given us in the Bible, He used men and women throughout scripture in ways that very rarely—if ever—made sense to the human mind.

> **God isn't concerned with making sense to you and me. He is concerned about us partnering with His plan. We aren't called to understand. We're called to trust and obey.**

God told Abraham to take his only son up a mountain and kill him. This was the promised son Abraham had been believing for. Abraham was 100 years old when Isaac was born, so I imagine Abraham didn't think that what God asked him to do made a lot of sense. However, Abraham had a history with God. God had already told Abraham to pack up, get away from his father's country, and go to a land God would show him later. Packing up everything you own and leaving for an unknown destination doesn't make a whole lot of sense either, but Abraham did it. So, with that history in mind, Abraham climbed the mountain with Isaac.

God told the prophet Hosea, "You see that prostitute down there? Go marry her." Hosea obeyed. However, she left him to go back to her life of prostitution. What God told Hosea next didn't make much sense either: God told him, "Go get her and bring her back home." When Hosea obeyed God, other people probably told him he was crazy. But, it was part of God's plan and purpose, and Hosea did what God said.

God is not concerned about making sense to us. He is concerned about us partnering with His plan. We aren't called to understand; we are called to trust and obey.

Our Lack of Past Experience Does Not Disqualify Us

God may also call you to do something you've never done before. Noah had never built an ark. In fact, we don't have any biblical evidence of Noah building *anything* before, let alone a large-scale construction project like this massive boat. Yet, God did not consult Noah's résumé. He simply called Noah to build the ark that would save the human race. Like Noah, God may use you to do something you've never done before.

God is not concerned about your past experience when He calls you to your future destination.

Noah wasn't qualified to build the ark on his own. However, since God called him, God also equipped him. God may very well call you to do things in a season of your life you've never done. When God calls you, perhaps you are trembling with fear and saying, "God, I've never done anything like that before." Maybe God is calling you to teach or lead or help in a life group and you say, "I've never done anything like that before." Maybe He's calling you out of your comfort zone to be an influence in a teenager's or a child's life and you respond, "I've never done anything like that before."

Know this: God is calling each believer into a season of building His Kingdom and building other people's lives. We don't earn or qualify for the calling He has for us. Actually, His call *is* the qualification for His plans.

We need to stop coming up with excuses and looking for reasons to disqualify ourselves from partnering with God. Instead, our response should be an immediate, "Yes. If You are calling me to it, I say, *yes Lord*." God will equip you when you say "yes." If God is calling you to something you don't feel prepared for, that means He already has a plan in place to prepare you. He is going to send you the people and the resources, He is going to bring you the support, and He is going to ensure you have everything else you need. Just because you don't have it right now, doesn't mean you won't have it when you need it. In fact, if you already have it, it's not God—it's just a good idea.

If God is calling you to something you don't feel prepared for, that means He already has a plan in place to prepare you.

God Calls, God Equips

God may even call you to do something no one has ever

29

done. Noah had never built an ark—but that wasn't all. *No one* had ever built an ark. He didn't have Wikipedia to see how the last guy built it. He didn't have anything to check—no source to go to. He was casting the mold and stepping out into rare territory by obeying what God called him to. There was no other pattern. There was only the pattern that God gave him.

I want you to know God is still raising up and calling risk takers, trail blazers, pioneers, world changers, and visionaries who know nothing else except to listen to God and do what He says. In so doing, they change the world. I firmly believe there are many of you reading this book that God is calling to do something that no one in your family—or even your community—has ever done.

In order to be the world changer God has called you to be, you can't look around and say, "I sense God is calling me to do this, but that's different from the things the generations before me have done. I'm going to be out here alone if I do that." Being alone can be a *good* thing because you don't have to worry about trying to keep up with and be like anybody else. You just follow what God tells you to do; do it in obedience, and it will change your world. It may even change everyone's world. The calling of God is upon all our lives to be a builder and a world changer!

Why Call Noah?

What were the circumstances in Noah's life that led God to call Noah to build the ark? Was he doing something out of the ordinary that caused God to call him, instead of someone else?

Genesis 6:9 gives us the answer, "Noah walked with God." What does that mean? He was in regular conversation with the Lord, walking with Him daily—and God used that fellowship time they had already established to speak to Noah. The call came out of the walk. Another way to say it is that the call came from the communion Noah had with God. I'm not talking about the communion we take when we eat the bread and drink from the cup. I'm talking about their common union, their fellowship, their walk one with the other.

God is more concerned about your daily walk than He is about your massive call because you can't perform and fulfill the call if you don't already have the walk.

If you and I would just focus on *walking with God*, we would *hear from God*. When we focus on a daily walk with God, we receive and perceive the call from God upon our lives. We need to focus on enjoying God's presence and walking with Him. Make space for Him. Give him room in your day and your life, and not just one room and one time. Don't just make one appointment. Give him space and a room and a drawer. I have serious concerns about people who say they have a call from God, yet they don't have a daily walk with Him.

The call comes out of the walk. It's that simple. God is more concerned with your daily walk than He is about your massive call. You can't perform and fulfill the call if you don't already have the walk.

Before God ever revealed His call to Noah, Noah first had a daily walk with God. Before there were any negative circumstances, Noah chose to walk with God (Genesis 6:9). Because he chose to walk with God when no one else was walking with God, God said, "Here is a man I can trust with a call." Think about it: Noah wasn't trying to get a word about a boat when God gave him a word about a boat. He was just walking with God. He didn't say, "I really need to hear from the Lord about this ark thing." No, he was just enjoying fellowship with the Lord. Out of the daily flow of his fellowship with God, God spoke to him about what was to come.

"How do I hear from God?"

I hear this question all the time. Most people make it seem complicated. The answer, though, is actually very simple. Just walk with God and build a relationship with Him on a daily basis. Over the years, I've noticed in my personal life that whenever I desperately needed to hear from the Lord, if I focused on trying to get clear direction, I didn't get it. Clarity came when I stopped thinking about the direction I needed and focused on the Lord. Actually, some of the times I received the clearest direction were when I was on vacation—when I didn't have anything pressing on my mind. It often happened when I was walking along the beach and admiring the day. Out of nowhere, God would start telling me His plan.

"The steps of a good man are ordered by Me, just like you are walking on this beach," He said to me one day. "I want you to get an understanding of the path I am going to order, so the steps of My people will grow, start changing lives, and shaping the culture in your area."

I said, "Well, Lord, that's wonderful. What's that going to look like?"

All of a sudden, God started speaking to me, and in the course of about twenty minutes, He gave me what I had been searching for during the previous three years. I heard God's voice, because I was just enjoying being with Him and fellow-shipping with Him.

God spoke to me in much the same way concerning marriage. I'd been wondering for a long time about getting married. I didn't know if I was supposed to have somebody in my life or if God wanted me to be alone. I was getting really frustrated, so I put it out of my mind. I decided I was going to trust God and enjoy His presence. When I put finding a wife out of my mind and concentrated on walking with the Lord, God brought the person into my life He wanted me to spend the rest of my life with.

Stop striving in your flesh to hear God!

So, what am I telling you? Quit striving in the flesh to hear from God. Simply enjoy God and be in His presence. In Psalm 46:10, God tells us to "Be still and know that I am God." Come back to the enjoyment of worship and prayer and shake off the labor and the striving in the flesh that will rob you of the joy of a close relationship with God. Just be still.

What we're doing, unintentionally, is turning time with God

into a means to an end to get what we want. We keep manipulating and trying to get everything from Him, but there is no real fellowship.

God's desire has always been to have fellowship with His people and see them become all that He designed them to be in His Kingdom.

"And I will be your Father, and you will be my sons and daughters," says the Lord Almighty. (2 Corinthians 6:18 NLT)

"The Call to Build" Key Points

Review these key points and begin to understand God's call on your life.

• God doesn't build your calling based on your circumstances. He builds your circumstances based on your calling.

• Because God had your calling in mind, He knew what family, community, generation, time, and skill set you would need to complete it.

• God isn't concerned with making sense to you and me. He is concerned about us partnering with His plan. We aren't called to understand. We're called to trust and obey.

• God is not concerned about your past experience when He calls you to your future destination.

The Call to Build Action Steps

Read the suggested action steps and check them off as you complete them.

* Stop trying to make sense out of what God has called you to. Your job is to obey God and move out and do what God is calling you to do. If you wait until it makes sense, you are never going to be living in obedience to God.

* Stop using the excuse that you are not prepared as a reason for not stepping into the call of God on your life. If God is calling you to something you do not feel prepared for that means He

already has a plan of how to prepare you.

* Stop striving and focus on a more intimate daily relationship with God. He's more concerned about your daily walk with Him than He is about your massive call, because you can't perform the call if you don't have the walk.

* Quit striving in the flesh to hear from God. Just enjoy God and being in His presence. Come back to the enjoyment of worship and prayer. Shake off the labor and the striving in the flesh and all those things that are trying to rob the joy of a close relationship with God.

* Describe the call you believe God has on your life.

Chapter 3

Blood, Sweat, and Tears

Thus Noah did; according to all that God commanded him, so he did. Then the Lord said to Noah, "Come into the ark, you and all your household, because I have seen that you are righteous before Me in this generation. You shall take with you seven each of every clean animal, a male and his female; two each of animals that are unclean, a male and his female; also seven each of birds of the air, male and female, to keep the species alive on the face of all the earth. For after seven more days I will cause it to rain on the earth forty days and forty nights, and I will destroy from the face of the earth all living things that I have made." And Noah did according to all that the Lord commanded him. Noah was six hundred years old when the floodwaters were on the earth. So Noah, with his sons, his wife, and his sons' wives, went into the ark because of the waters of the flood. Of clean animals, of animals that are unclean, of birds, and of everything that creeps on the earth, two by two they went into the ark to Noah, male and female, as God had commanded Noah. And it came to pass after seven days that the waters of the flood were on the earth. In the six hundredth year of Noah's life, in the second month, the seventeenth day of the month, on that day all the fountains of the great deep were broken up, and the windows of heaven were opened. (Genesis 6:22-7:11)

Many people wrestle with how long it took to build the ark, because the Bible does not explicitly say. The general consensus is that it took somewhere around seventy-five years. That's a long time to build a boat. But remember, this wasn't your average boat. This was a boat that would change the world. It was a large-scale project.

The Hoover Dam took five years to build. Mt. Rushmore took fourteen. The Panama Canal took the French and Americans a total of thirty-four years to build. Keep in mind, that was with all the modern-day technology and resources available at the time. Even with hundreds and thousands of people, these projects still took years and years to complete. When you understand that those massive projects were not overnight undertakings—and you realize Noah and his sons did not have modern technology—then seventy-five years to build the ark seems reasonable.

The construction of the ark was not a quick work. There was a process. There was a season that took place between the time God called Noah to build and the time the boat was ready to withstand the coming storm. Some people know that God has called them to build and begin to focus on the building process. They are often passionate in the beginning. But, between the call and the completion is a season that may last longer than they anticipated.

Noah didn't walk away from his prayer time with God and then suddenly the ark appears. As much as God wanted the ark built, He didn't give Noah a ready-built boat. What He gave Noah was a call and a plan. God didn't send angels to build the boat for Noah. Noah had to build it himself. Noah had to do the work of building the boat. He had to invest seventy-five years of blood, sweat, and tears.

It's an amazing feeling when you first realize what God is calling you to build. You get excited and passionately rush ahead to get started. Then you have a second realization: that you have to *actually build it yourself*. It's wonderful when God calls you to build a godly marriage and family, but you have to build it. God isn't going to build it for you. He isn't going to send angels to build it for you. Your family, your pastor, and your leaders can't build it for you. No one else can build it for you. Just like Noah, you have to put in the blood, sweat, and tears to build it yourself.

There isn't going to be a heavenly bailout program that spares you the effort of building what God calls you to build. Between the call and the completion, there is a building season that all of us have to go through.

There isn't going to be a heavenly bailout program that spares you the effort of building what God calls you to build.

Here's the truth about the building season: while Noah was building the ark, God was building Noah. While you're building that godly family, God is building you. While you're building your education, God is building you. The building season is something we all have to go through. The fact is, though, most people don't make it through the building season. Cemeteries are full of people who gave up in the middle of their building seasons. Oh, they were excited about the call to build and they were passionate in the beginning; because the call to build is awesome, but the process of building is not.

We all need that moment that gives us the clarity of the call to build. But then, we get in the building season and most people phase out. They fall by the wayside, and never complete what God called them to build. Chances are, your building season won't last seventy-five years like Noah's. But, whatever it is God calls you to build, it's not going to happen overnight. It's going to take some time and you need to be equipped to survive the building season.

Surviving the Building Season

There are three things we all need to make it through the building season: vision, focus, and patience.

If you don't know where you're going, you won't know when you get there.

We must have vision. You have to see it in your mind before you'll see it in reality. You need to see the finished product God is calling you to build. If you don't know where you're going, you won't know when you get there.

For example, if God is calling you to build a godly family, you need a vision of what that would look like in your household. You would need to sit down with your spouse and kids and have a conversation about your vision. Wishful thinking isn't enough to ensure your family all receives Jesus. Each family member can't have his or her own definition of what the end product should look like. You must have a vision of what God is calling you to build so you are in unity and are all moving in the same direction. God says we are to be people of vision.

Where there is no vision my people perish. (Proverbs 29:18)

Everyone who was not in the boat with Noah perished, because they didn't have the vision Noah had. God is saying, "if you don't have vision for what I'm calling you to build, you'll never get past the call." You'll never make it to completion, because the building season will require you to be a visionary. So many challenges and obstacles will come against you in the building season that if you don't know *where* you're going, or if you do not know *why* you're doing what you're doing, you'll give up in the middle of the building season.

If you don't have vision for what God is calling you to build, you'll never get past the call.

Write the vision and make it plain on tablets, that he may run who reads it. (Habakkuk 2:2)

It's not enough to simply have the vision, you need to write the vision down. Then, what does God want you to do with the vision? He says you need to *run* with it—not crawl with it. You are to make progress with it and move forward with God's vision. Saying, "I'll pray about it" becomes the camouflage for inaction. Once you have God's vision for your career, you need to write it down. Once you have the vision for your personal life, you need to write it down. Once you have God's vision for your family and your marriage, you need to write it down. Don't trust your memory! This is too important.

But, why is it so important? If you don't have God's vision for your life, everyone around you is going to have *their* vision for your life. Their vision is never going to be the vision you want and—more importantly—it's not going to be the vision God wants.

If you don't have God's vision for your life, everyone around you is going to have their vision for your life.

That's why when you walk into our church in Pikeville, Kentucky, the focal point of our atrium is our mission statement. Each time we come together, we're reminded of what God has called us to do. We aren't going to take the chance or leave it to our memory and hope that we're going in the right direction. We want to have it written down so everybody God calls to be part of this church family knows where we're going and why we exist. We aren't leaving the vision of God up for grabs in hopes someone can lead us the right direction. We know what God has called us to do and I want to make sure we are all moving forward in the same direction. So, remember: as you are moving from call to completion, you have to (1) have the vision and (2) write it down.

We can't allow the actions or inactions of other people to cause us to stop building. We must have focus.

We must have focus. We can't allow the actions or inactions of other people to distract us or stop us from building what God has called us to build. Noah's building season lasted seventy-five years. At the beginning of the season, he and his boys were the only ones building. At the end of the season, he and the boys were still the only ones building. I can imagine Noah waking up one morning around year forty-two and saying: "I'm a little discouraged. I've been building this boat for forty-two years and no one has lifted a finger to help me. So, I'm gonna sit down and stop building until someone else gets ready to build." If he'd done that, then the ark wouldn't have been built.

We can't allow the actions or inactions of other people to cause us to stop building or to blur our focus. God called Noah to build; and Noah needed to keep building until God told him to stop. The only time to stop building is when you get to completion and the vision is realized. Noah built for seventy-five years. He endured much persecution and received little support—but *he kept building.*

The only time to stop building is when you get to completion and the vision is realized.

When you're in your building season, you'll come up against a multitude of distractions and have excuses as to why you should stop building. But, the fact is the *only* one who can un-call you from building is the one who called you to build in the first place. He isn't going to tell you to stop until your boat is finished. Keep building. Often, God's call will require persistence in the midst of persecution. It will require motivation in the midst of mockery. You must keep building. Don't let anybody do anything to cause you to stop building what God called you to build.

I recently came home with a bird feeder. It's shaped like a little narrow house and it hangs from our roof line. I didn't realize when the bird feeder was hung, it would call the International Squirrel Convention to meet outside. Do you remember the squirrel in the Disney movie "The Emperor's New Groove?" It just kept squeaking. That's what was going on outside our home all day long. Every day. Squeak. Squeak! SQUEAK!!

As I sat looking at the squirrels one day, I noticed one in particular that was fixated on the bird feeder. He smelled the bird seed and decided he just had to have it. The bird feeder was located between the gutter and the motion light. It looked impossible for this squirrel to get to the food. But, this brave little squirrel was the MacGyver or Jack Bauer of squirrels. He was determined to get that bird seed. He was focused. He climbed up the metal gutter, which was a feat in and of itself. When he made it to the top, he had another problem: birds (the intended recipients of the seed buffet) were landing on the feeder, eating their fill, then taking off. The bird traffic caused the feeder to swing to and fro. With this newly discovered obstacle, the squirrel decided he couldn't make the jump directly onto the bird feeder. But that realization didn't stop him. He just decided on a new course of action to accomplish his vision. With his original plan thwarted, the squirrel decided he could jump *past* the bird feeder and onto the motion light fixture—so he did. But, once he jumped to the motion light, he realized that wasn't where he wanted to be. So, back to gutter he went. This tenacious squirrel tried several times, but just couldn't turn his vision into reality.

Then, he decided to give it one last try. He put his back feet on the gutter and tried to reach the feeder by stretching out to his full length. But, it was still too far. After all else failed, the squirrel mustered up all the courage he had in his little rodent body, threw caution to the wind, and jumped off the gutter onto the swinging bird feeder. He grabbed onto the front of it with his front paws and swung his back paws onto the back side of it. The squirrel was now hanging upside down underneath the feeder, holding on for dear life.

He could smell the bird seed. He could almost taste it. What he couldn't do was *reach* it. If he let go, he would fall. It took some doing, but he finally jumped back onto the gutter. At this point, most of us would have given up. We had a vision—but we'd tried, right? Time to pack it up and head home. But, not this little guy. He finally figured out that if he jumped *sideways* onto the bird feeder, he could achieve his goal. When he did, he looked ridiculous with one foot up in the air propped on the roof of the bird feeder and the other three balancing him. He lay there in the most awkward position and buried his face in the bird food. He gorged himself like we do when we go to an all-you-can-eat buffet.

This whole drama took about thirty or forty minutes to unfold. I sat there watching this determined little squirrel thinking, "*that* is focus." This is a squirrel that tried and failed and tried and failed again. But he didn't let that stop him. He kept trying until he got what he was after. Unfortunately, that squirrel was more focused than many of us who would climb to the gutter of what God is calling us to do and we say, "Well, I tried, but I can't do it." Then, we go find something else to do—something *we* decide will be a better use of our time.

When God calls you to build, have persistent focus and don't stop until you move to the completion. Because His purpose doesn't stop with you. It extends to His other children, maybe even yours. Your part has to be complete so that theirs can begin.

We need to move through our building season with an understanding that patience is endurance with a purpose.

We must have patience. Sometimes when we think about patience, we think it means standing in line and not cussing somebody out—or that it means being in the doctor's office and waiting a long time without constantly complaining to the receptionist. Don't get me wrong. Not losing your temper as you stand in the never-ending, glacially-slow line at Walmart should definitely be part of your prayer target. But, there's more to patience than being able to stand in a long line. We need to move through our building season with an understanding that patience is endurance with a purpose.

Patience isn't just waiting; patience is waiting with a purpose. Patience is knowing that you're in your building season and it isn't going to come cheap and it isn't going to come easy. It's knowing that it will take some time to build the family, marriage, ministry, or business God is calling you to build. Patience is knowing it isn't going to happen overnight.

Patience means that when the obstacles and the challenges come, you look back to your vision and stay focused. You can keep going because not only did God call you to build, He also told you what to build. You can keep going and put hammer to nail—even if you're building all by yourself. You can keep building day after day, resistance after resistance, obstacle after obstacle, persecution after persecution, and ridicule after ridicule. You can keep building and have patience through the process—all because you have a vision from God.

Good Planning and Hard Work

Good planning and hard work lead to prosperity, but hasty shortcuts lead to poverty. (Proverbs 21:5 NLT)

Everything worth doing is worth doing right. To reach prosperity you need both good planning and hard work. First you need good planning—the vision. Then, hard work brings the prosperity. The church world is notorious for praying and getting the vision, but failing to put in the hard work when it comes to building. We'll pray all day long about it until we know what needs to be done. Then, six months later, we're still praying about it. Or maybe we delegate the task to a committee—where visions go to die. In Noah's life, there came a time when he had to stop praying about the ark and start building it.

There are some things in your life that you know God has called you to do. You've prayed about it, you've put a committee on it, but now you need to build it. You know God is calling you to build that marriage and that family, so quit waiting around for someone else to come in and save the day. Build what God is telling you to build!

If I'd been Noah, somewhere around year sixty-seven, I'd be thinking, "there has to be a faster way. Can't somebody go to Lowes and get some power tools? Maybe we can get Chip and Joanna Gaines in here to move this thing along. Can't get them? Okay, I'll settle for Handy Manny—he seemed like he was doing a good job on the Disney Channel with that talking hammer. We've got to get this thing done." It's normal for us to want to hurry God along. It's normal for us to want to move this process ahead a little faster. When we do something for a long time and nothing happens, we want to find short cuts to help God out. But, the Word tells us when we get hasty and try to find short-cuts, it leads us to poverty. When we cut corners, we end up with nothing at all—or we end up with something that looks nothing like the vision God originally gave us.

You see enthusiasts building their model cars or those ships in a bottle that require craftsmanship and patience with every tiny, intricate detail. But, we often build our lives haphazardly when what you and I are building is much more serious than a model car. We understand patience, not getting in a hurry, and following the instructions when building those things. But when it comes to building the life God has called us to build, we keep asking how long it's going to take. Like a small child on a road trip, we ask over and over, "Are we there yet?" We want to hurry up and find a shortcut.

The Word tells us when we get hasty and try to find shortcuts, it leads us to poverty.

It takes some time as you walk through your building season, but you're not alone. God's Spirit is right here with you—guiding you, equipping you, and empowering you to build what He is calling you to build. When you put in your blood, sweat, and tears, God will take you through to completion.

Blood, Sweat, and Tears Key Points

• There isn't going to be a heavenly bailout program that spares you the effort of building what God calls you to build.

• If you don't know where you're going, you won't know when you get there.

• If you don't have vision for what God is calling you to build, you'll never get past the call.

• We can't allow the actions or inactions of other people to cause us to stop building. We must have focus.

• The only time to stop building is when you get to completion and the vision is realized.

• We need to move through our building season with an understanding that patience is endurance with a purpose.

• The Word tells us when we get hasty and try to find shortcuts, it leads us to poverty.

Blood, Sweat, and Tears Action Steps

Read the suggested action steps and check them off as you complete them. Add your own as the Lord continues to instruct you.

* Do you know where you are going? Do you see the finished product that God is calling you to build? If you cannot see it, how will you know when you get there? Write down your vision.

* Are you allowing the actions or inactions of other people to cause you to stop building? If you are, then you need to be focused on the vision and get your focus off of them.

* Has God told you to stop building? Then keep building until you get to completion and the vision is realized.

* When God calls you to build, have persistent focus and do not stop until you move to the completion of what God has called you to build. Make this firm commitment today.

* Good planning and hard work lead to prosperity, but hasty shortcuts, lead to poverty. Which will you choose?

Chapter 4

Surviving the Storm

*Then the Lord said to Noah, "Come into the ark, you and all
your household, because I have seen that you are righteous before
Me in this generation. You shall take with you seven each of every
clean animal, a male and his female; two each of animals that are
unclean, a male and his female; also seven each of birds of the air,
male and female, to keep the species alive on the face of all the
earth. For after seven more days I will cause it to rain on the earth
forty days and forty nights, and I will destroy from the face of the
earth all living things that I have made." **And Noah did
according to all that the LORD commanded him.***
(Genesis 7:1-5 emphasis added)

Unfortunately, we're all going to encounter life's storms—
they're unavoidable. No doubt, you're acquainted with those
seasons when serenity and peace leaves to be replaced by clouds
of trouble and heartache. There's no pill we can swallow, no
silver bullet we can buy, no book we can read, and not even a
scripture or prayer we can recite that will prevent storms. Not
money, not talent, not education, and not even following Jesus
will abate the storms of life.

**Jesus said the storms will come, but we can be pre-
served and survive every storm.**

*"These things I have spoken to you, that in Me you may have
peace. In the world you will have tribulation; but be of good cheer,
I have overcome the world." (John 16:33)*

Jesus said storms will come. They are a reality; but, just like with Noah, the storm doesn't have to destroy us. We can be preserved, and we can survive every storm.

Notice that the storm Noah was about to experience wasn't because of his own actions or his own choices. Noah was in the storm due to the actions and choices of everyone else around him. Noah was in the storm because of other people's sins, other people's rebellion, and other people's disobedience. Noah isn't the only person in scripture to experience a storm that wasn't due to his own actions.

For instance, let's look at the story of Jonah. There were some men who had a fishing business. They were just going about another day on the job, and a backslidden preacher shows up and says, "I need to hitch a ride." He pays the fare to get in the boat and they are going about a normal day. Suddenly, a hurricane comes up and they are fighting for their lives. These fishermen hadn't rebelled against God. But, they found them-selves in the middle of storm because somebody in their boat was disobedient.

It's just a fact of life: the people we love and to whom we are closest sometimes bring storms into our lives. Noah was going through a storm because others had sinned. God declared Noah's righteousness. The interesting thing here is that Noah didn't shake his fist toward the heavens and say, "God, this isn't fair. I shouldn't have to go through this storm. I'm righteous. *You* declared I'm righteous. It's not right. It doesn't make sense that I'm going through this." Noah didn't blame other people for his storm—he just simply built what God told him to build.

The reality is, we'll run out of people to blame.

Blame or Build?

The storms will come, but we have a choice to make. We can spend our limited time on this earth doing one of two things: we blame other people for our storms *or* we can build the life God wants us to build and build God's Kingdom. If you spend your energy blaming people for the storms, that's energy you can't spend building the life God has called you to build. Besides, you'll eventually run out of other people to blame.

This is a difficult truth for us to hear—much less to receive and apply to our lives. In our present-day generation, it's popular to blame everybody else for the storms we experience. We don't own up to our shortcomings. We have models and examples of shifting blame to others all around us. It's bred into us: everywhere we look, we see a blaming culture. That culture tells us it's everybody else's fault that our lives turned out like they did. Many of us have not built the family, marriage, home, or career God wants us to build because we have spent all our time and energy blaming other people for our storms. Each of us has a limited amount of time, energy, and strength in our life. We must spend it wisely.

That's our culture; but, the truth is, it's not a new concept. In fact, the blame game goes all the way back to the Garden of Eden. When a storm called sin came upon the horizon and the curse entered the world, God showed up to confront the man and the woman. The blame shifting started immediately.

Eve said it was the serpent's fault. Adam started out saying it was Eve's fault, but then he went on to say, "Actually God, if we really want to be honest about who gets the blame, let's look at the situation. God, it's really *your* fault because everything was fine until you gave me this woman. It's the woman that *you gave me*, God. You and I were fine. We were tight. Everything was great here in the Garden. Then *you* gave me *her*. If you hadn't given me this woman, I wouldn't have eaten the fruit. I wouldn't be in this situation. It's Eve's fault, it's the devil's fault, and, God, it's *your* fault!"

All these years and generations later, we are still trying to find somebody to blame. We think: "Why am I in a financial storm? It is everybody else's fault. Why am I in a marriage storm? It is everybody else's fault. Why is my family so messed up? It is everybody else's fault."

You can blame, or you can build—but you can't do both. You can spend your time trying to find somebody else to blame for the storm or you can spend your time building the life God has called you to build. The choice is yours.

The Holy Spirit has anointed us to be builders—not to be blamers.

You are anointed to build a godly life, a godly home, a godly business, and a godly family. God has called you to build—not to find somebody else to blame for your storm. Be more focused on the calling and the solution than the problem and the fault.

A Life-Changing Storm

What kind of storm was Noah facing? Noah and his family weren't going to experience a little April shower. This wasn't a cloud burst. They were about to experience a life-changing storm—a *world*-changing storm. Have you ever been in a storm that would change your life, your family, and your everyday existence?

Noah and his family experienced a storm that came at them from every direction. Genesis 1 says God established an ocean of water above the earth. During the flood, it all came crashing down. The fountains of the great deep opened up and there were volcanic eruptions from subterranean reservoirs that came shooting up from under the earth. Then the winds and waves began rocking and shaking the ark from side to side. If that wasn't enough, for the first time ever, it started to rain. For forty days and forty nights, the rain didn't let up.

Maybe you haven't experienced a storm of life like Noah's yet—a storm that seems never-ending and alters your reality. However, the moment will probably come when your life is forever changed by a storm so strong that it becomes a defining moment. Just like everything in the world changed because of Noah's storm, everything in your world will be different because of your storm.

Noah didn't go into the storm unprepared.

God prepared Noah for the storm that would change every-thing. God knew the storm was coming, so He prepared Noah. You may go into a storm that feels like it's coming at you from every direction and will change everything in your life. But your God is not a cruel, abusive, or negligent Father. He won't send you into a storm that He hasn't already prepared you for and equipped you to survive.

In Noah's case, we know God had been talking about the flood for at least 120 years before it came. For seventy-five years, God nudged Noah—speaking to him, guiding him, and instructing him, saying, "Noah, here's what you need to do to get ready for this flood." Noah listened and was obedient to God, so he was prepared to survive the storm.

Just like with Noah, God is instructing, speaking, nudging, preparing, and equipping *you* every day. He knows the storms you're going to come up against tomorrow, next week, next year, and ten years from now. He knows what storm is ahead of you and He's not going to allow you to go into a storm that He hasn't prepared you for.

In preparation for the storm, God told Noah he needed to build a boat. However, God didn't leave it up to Noah what kind of boat he ought to build. He had specific plans for Noah to weather his storm—and He has specific plans for you to weather your storm.

God is instructing, speaking, nudging, preparing, and equipping *you* every day.

God Gives Us the Blueprints

God has a blueprint for everything He's called you to build.

God didn't say to Noah, "There's going to be a storm—a *lot* of water—and it would probably be a good idea if you built a boat. You just figure it out and build what you think would be best for the storm."

God was precise about the kind of boat Noah needed to build. In Genesis 6:14-16, God gave Noah the blueprints for the boat. In United States standard measurements, Noah's ark would be 510 feet long, 85 feet wide, and 51 feet tall. God was specific in giving Noah the blueprint for what He called Noah to build.

God calls all of us to be builders and He has a blueprint for everything. God has a blueprint for a godly life, marriage, home, and business. God even has a blueprint for what government, finances, and the economy should look like. Simply put, anything and everything we're called and anointed to build, God already has the blueprint for us in His Word.

Why was God so specific with Noah? God knew the boat Noah needed to build, because God knew the storm Noah was going to experience. I don't know what kind of storms I'm going to face in my life—but God does. I don't even know what I'm going to face tomorrow—but God does. He is preparing me for tomorrow's storm today and He is showing me what I need to build today what I will need for the coming storm. If I will just obey God and do what God is telling me to build today, I will survive whatever may come at me tomorrow. He won't send me into a storm unprepared. And He won't send you into your storm unprepared, either. His anchor is stronger than any storm. If we are rooted in Him and His design, we will come out of the storm alive. Maybe battered and bruised with damage to our belongings, but alive and well with a renewed knowledge that we are held in the hands of the Creator.

While there's a specific design and blueprint for whatever God is calling you to build in His Word, society pressures you to make modifications. For example, God's Word contains the blueprint for marriage, but our generation wants to change that blueprint. If we concede and modify God's blueprint for marriage in our lives, it unfolds everything else that God has established a blueprint and pattern for. When we modify one blueprint, we continue to drift and fall away from God's pattern and blueprint in our lives.

Don't Modify God's Design

When you're in that long building season and you're building according to God's blueprint, it's easy to be tempted to change God's design. At some point, you're going to think you know better than God what the pattern ought to be. You're going to think that you know how to build your life better than God does. And, when you entertain those thoughts, you'll be tempted to think you know how to build your marriage, family, business, career, education, and finances better than God. How arrogant can we become?

When we build what God tells us to build by His design, we'll survive any storm.

Jesus taught us about the importance of building according to God's design in Matthew Chapter 7. There, Jesus said there were two men building their houses. One of the men built his house on the sand, while the other built an identical house—but he built his on the rock. Jesus explained that if we hear what He's saying and follow His directions, then we are like the wise man who built his house on the rock. When the storm comes and beats down upon your house on the rock, it stands solid—it's preserved, and it overcomes the storm. But, when we hear what Jesus is saying and fail to follow His directions, we're like the man who built his house on the sand. Remember, it's the *same* house that was built on the rock. But, it wasn't built according to God's plan. If the same storm comes along the house on the rock weathered, it will destroy the house we built on the sand. Even though we did *what* God told us to, we didn't do it *how* He told us to.

You can see this in the Word of God and you can see it in history. You can have two people, two families, two homes, and two marriages that go through the same storm. One makes it and the other doesn't. Why? Because one was built according to God's pattern and the other wasn't. When we build what God tells us to build, how God tells us to build it, we'll survive any storm.

As a pastor, I read books. I go to conferences. I have overseers and mentors and counselors. But, ultimately, the best way to build a church is according to God's blueprint. He has a blueprint for everything and we need to build accordingly. God gave Noah a very detailed plan for the ark—and what was

Noah's response to God's blueprint? Genesis 6:22 says Noah did all that God commanded. Then, when God told Noah the storm was on its way in Genesis 7:5, 9, and 16, the Word says time and again, *"Noah did all that Lord commanded him."* And, what was the result of Noah's obedience? Noah survived the storm because he built according to God's plan.

Obey God Before and During the Storm

Here's what Noah's story teaches us: we can't allow the gathering clouds of the storm to change our focus. Noah walked with God before he knew about a storm. He kept walking with God and obeying God before the storm, and he continued to obey God in the midst of the storm. In the stormy seasons of life, we need to come back to the fundamental and basic things. I have observed over the course of several years that people don't tend to follow Noah's example when storms come. Here are four common reactions to life's storms:

1. Respond out of fear rather than faith. People who respond to the storm from a place of fear rather than faith are afraid they're going to lose everything. They make bad decisions and do crazy things because they're responding out of fear. They listen to the wrong voices. Other people will always tell you what *they* think *you* need to do. Chances are, the people who are being vocal in your storm aren't the people you should listen to. People who have been married and divorced more times than Elizabeth Taylor will try to coach you on what you need to do through your marriage storm. You don't need that! What you need is to get alone with God and His Word and say, "God, I need Your blueprint. I need Your voice and Your direction to tell me what You want me to do to get through this storm."

2. Second-guess God. If we begin to second-guess God when the storm comes, we think things like, "Did I really hear God tell me to build the boat? Maybe God said, 'wait for the dog to bark,' rather than 'build an ark.'" We start to doubt the things we were so sure of prior to the storm. If that's where you are, you're not alone. In fact, that was the first tactic Satan used when he spoke to Eve in the Garden. He said to Eve, "Did God *really* say you shouldn't eat that fruit?" When the pressure is on, the enemy tries to get you to second guess what God has said in your life.

3. Try to figure it out without God. When you're in the middle of the storm, you may try to get through it with your strength and ability—you may try to figure it out and deal with it yourself. You may think, "When I get through this trouble, I'll get back to God." Remember when the disciples were in the storm? They thought they were going to die and started frantically bailing water. But they couldn't get to the other side of that storm by their own strength or ability. When you're in the middle of a storm, it isn't the time to try to prove how smart, well-connected, or business savvy you are. You need Jesus in the storm—just like the disciples did. He's the only one who knows how to calm not only you, but also the storm that's all around you.

4. Try to open a door God has shut. The Lord closed the door behind Noah and his family once they were in the ark. God's way of keeping them safe from the storm was closing a door. If you have a door suddenly close in your life, it's not fun. But, if you could look back with God's perspective, you'd see what God sees on the other side of that closed door. Many times in my life, I've tried to make things happen for myself. And often, I get a ways down the road with what I think was a good result and I finally stop to pray about it. God's answer is always the same. "That was cute, but watch this." And anything He orchestrates is ten thousand times better than the way I tried to pave for myself. Closing the door was God's way of keeping you safe from a storm that lay just on the other side. Because we're stubborn, bull-headed, and disobedient, we can get stuck in a rut. God knows the only way you're going to get out of that ungodly, unhealthy job or relationship is for Him to slam a door in your face. When God shuts the door, don't do what so many of us try to do—don't put your foot on the door and try and push it open.

Recently, I had something that I was praying through and seeking God about. I asked my leadership team to pray. We said, "Lord, if this isn't You, close this door in such a way that we know emphatically, and we'll walk away." I received a letter in the mail shortly after our prayer and that door was shut. Now what was my response? I was mad. I wanted to write a letter back saying I wasn't happy about it. But you know, after I calmed down over the course of a few days, I thanked God for shutting that door. I believe on the other side was a storm that we had no idea we would've gotten in the middle of. I said to God, "You saw the flood and the storm coming over there and You wanted to preserve us from the storm. You just shut the door. Thank you, Father." Sometimes, we pray for God to open a door when the best thing that can happen is for God to shut it instead.

Because Noah and his family were faithful to God and they built what God told them to build, in the manner God told them to build it, they were safe in the storm. Things may come against us, but if we are faithful and obedient to the Word of God, He promises us that it will stay outside. It won't come inside and affect who we are. This is the kind of God you and I have. God doesn't just *preserve* us in the storm—He *promotes* us in the storm.

> *And the waters receded continually from the earth. At the end of the hundred and fifty days the waters decreased. Then the ark rested in the seventh month, the seventeenth day of the month, on the mountains of Ararat.* (Genesis 8:3-4)

Surviving the Storm Key Points

* Jesus said the storms will come, but we can be preserved and survive every storm.

* The Holy Spirit has anointed us to be builders—not to be blamers.

* Noah didn't go into the storm unprepared.

* God is instructing, speaking, nudging, preparing, and equipping you every day.

* God has a blueprint for everything He's called you to build.

* When we build what God tells us to build by His design, we'll survive any storm.

* God doesn't just *preserve* us in the storm—He *promotes* us in the storm.

Surviving the Storm *Action Steps*

Read the suggested action steps and check them off as you complete them. Add your own as the Lord continues to instruct you.

* It's been said there are three kinds of people in the world. Circle the group you are currently in.
Those who are about to go into a storm.
Those who are in a storm.
Those who are coming out of a storm.

* You can blame, or you can build—but you can't do both. Decide that you are not going to try to find somebody to blame. Instead, determine you are just going to be faithful to build what God has called you to build.

* What has God been instructing, speaking, nudging, preparing, and equipping you to do? Do it today, because He is preparing you for the storm to come.

* Don't respond to your storm out of fear rather than faith.

* Don't try to second-guess God.

* Don't try and figure it out without God.

* Don't be foolish and go back to try to open a door that God has shut.

* Obey God before and during the storm.

Chapter 5

Leave the Boat

So it came to pass, at the end of forty days, that Noah opened the window of the ark which he had made. Then he sent out a raven, which kept going to and fro until the waters had dried up from the earth. He also sent out from himself a dove, to see if the waters had receded from the face of the ground. But the dove found no resting place for the sole of her foot, and she returned into the ark to him, for the waters were on the face of the whole earth. So he put out his hand and took her, and drew her into the ark to himself. And he waited yet another seven days, and again he sent the dove out from the ark. Then the dove came to him in the evening, and behold, a freshly plucked olive leaf was in her mouth; and Noah knew that the waters had receded from the earth. (Genesis 8:6–11)

God told Noah the storm would last forty days and forty nights. He'd been counting down the days, and at the end of the fortieth night, Noah opened a window. He knew if God said forty days and forty nights, God *meant* forty days and forty nights. He held on to the Word of the Lord through the storm. That's what you and I have to do when we are in the storms of life. We have to hold on to God's Word through every storm. We have to be informed of the Word of God and build our life on what He has said. Then, when the storms come, we have to know that God has not changed His mind just because we're in the storm.

We are to hold onto the Word of God—just like Noah did. We are to take a step of faith, believing that God's Word is true, like Noah did when he opened the window. He believed that when he opened the window, rain was not going to blow in on his face. He believed when he opened that window, there would be no more storm. He was confident in these things because he believed God—and God said the storm would only last forty days.

If we really believe the Word of God, then we must take a step of faith in response to what God has said. We need to believe in and act on the promises of God. James said faith without works is dead (James 2:26). Maybe it's time for you to take a step of faith and act on the Word of God. Your actions—not just your words—need to demonstrate reliance on God's promises. We need to live out our lives as witnesses and demonstrate through actions taken in faith that we believe God's Word. We need to trust God to do greater things than He has ever done before in our lives when we take that step of faith. Maybe it is time you opened a window.

We need to let our lives demonstrate that we believe God's Word.

The Raven and the Dove

When Noah first opened the window, he sent out a raven. In Jewish custom, the raven was an unclean animal. Noah sent the raven out and it went to and fro and did nothing—it brought nothing back and accomplished nothing. This is a picture of what most of us do when we're in a storm: we rely upon our flesh to try and figure everything out on our own. We try to use our limited intelligence, strength, tenacity, and willpower to find our way through the storm.

> *Trust in the Lord with all your heart,*
> *And lean not on your own understanding;*
> *In all your ways acknowledge Him,*
> *And He shall direct your paths.* (Proverbs 3:5-6)

God tells us to trust in Him with all our hearts. We are not to lean on our own understanding, but, instead, to acknowledge God. If we do that, He will direct our paths, even when everything is beating us down and all of life is coming against us. When we lean upon ourselves and try to figure things out on our own, we're sending the raven out. The raven will always come back empty.

We have to break the pattern of sending the raven before the dove.

When the raven came back empty, Noah decided to send out the dove. In scripture, the dove is a symbol of the Holy Spirit. In your life, how many times do you only look to the dove after you've tried the raven first to no avail? When we do things in that order, we're not following the leading of the Lord. When we try everything else first and only then seek wise counsel from godly people, we're sending out the raven. When we decide we're just going to send out the raven and do it our way to get through the storm, we're not choosing God's best for our lives. After we do that time and again—and finally realize it's producing nothing—only then do we say, "Well, I guess I might as well send the dove out and maybe the Holy Spirit can give me the mind of Christ on what I'm supposed to do here." We have to break this pattern of sending the raven before the dove.

After the raven yielded no return, Noah decided to release the dove. Do you know what the dove brought back? Nothing. What Noah did next is an example of maturity we all need in our lives. *Noah sent the dove out again.*

The secret here is consistency. Noah said, "I'm going to send the dove one more time. I'm going to continue looking for the dove of the Holy Spirit to give me direction and guidance." The second time Noah sent the dove, the dove brought the answer—then Noah knew that the waters had receded from the earth.

We need to live under the direction and power of the Holy Spirit.

If you'll just let the dove loose in your life—and let the Holy Spirit really direct you—the Holy Spirit will give you the answer you need. The Bible says God's Word will not return to Him void, but it will accomplish the thing that He sends it to do (Isaiah 55:11). When we consistently have patience and follow the leading of the Holy Spirit, He will never leave us empty and without direction. Jesus promised the Holy Spirit would guide us into all truth (John 16:13). We need to live under the direction and power of the Holy Spirit.

Go Out of the Ark

Then God spoke to Noah, saying, "Go out of the ark, you and your wife, and your sons and your sons' wives with you. Bring out with you every living thing of all flesh that is with you: birds and cattle and every creeping thing that creeps on the earth, so that they may abound on the earth, and be fruitful and multiply on the earth." So Noah went out, and his sons and his wife and his sons' wives with him. Every animal, every creeping thing, every bird, and whatever creeps on the earth, according to their families, went out of the ark. (Genesis 8:15-19)

God told Noah to *build* the boat, and He told Noah to get *into* the boat—but then God told Noah to get *out* of the boat. Noah spent seventy-five years working on the ark to spend only a little over one year in it. On paper, that doesn't look like a very good investment. In 2016, the Ark Encounter theme park opened in Grant County, Kentucky. The ark depicted in the park is 510 feet long, 85 feet wide, and 51 feet high. Officials indicated the cost exceeded $100 million. That gives you some idea of the resources Noah would have invested into building the ark—and that's besides the seventy-five years of his life Noah poured into building the ark. If I told you that you need to spend seventy-five years and millions of dollars to build something that you're only going to spend thirteen months in, you'd say that isn't a good investment.

If we'd been Noah, many of us would've said, "But, God, seriously? I spent the last seventy-five years of my life building this ark and it only has one storm on it. We're just now breaking this thing in. You're telling me that after thirteen months—after just *one* storm—to just walk away from the thing that I spent seventy-five years building? You want me to just leave it behind?"

No matter your age, your past experience or how long you've been serving God, as long as there is breath in your body, God has a next season for you to move into.

As amazing and as world-changing as the construction and navigation of the ark was, God didn't leave Noah there. Noah's life wasn't concluded in the ark season. God had a new season for Noah to move into. God didn't just have a next season for Noah—He also has a next season for *you*. No matter your age, your past experience or how long you've been serving God, as long as there is breath in your body, God has a next season for you to move into.

To everything there is a season, a time for every purpose under heaven. (Ecclesiastes 3:1)

There may be times when you spend years building a job, a career or a business. Then, things come up and it's as if the voice of God tells you to leave the boat. At that moment, you must not allow your investment to become more predominant than God's call in your life. This one is hard. It's the master lesson in humility to step back and say I don't matter. I am irrelevant to this portion of God's plan. And that's ok. Because we are relevant to another part of the plan. We have to be in the right spot, operating in the right calling on the right purpose. If we are more focused on what we have invested in than what God is saying, we'll always be on the backside of what God is doing. So many people don't move into their next season because they are so focused on how much they have invested in building their boat. All the while, God is telling them there is a new season ready for them to move into. We can't focus on our investment and, in so doing, forfeit God's next season for our lives.

We can't focus on our investment and, in so doing, forfeit God's next season for our lives.

You can't allow a season of your life to define your life. God always has a next season for you. You can't camp out where God *has been*. You can't be content to be on the backside of the movement and the activity of God. You must not become so enamored in what you've invested in that you can't possibly fathom that it's time for you to move into a new season.

What Was Noah's Next Season?

Then Noah built an altar to the Lord, and took of every clean animal and of every clean bird, and offered burnt offerings on the altar. And the Lord smelled a soothing aroma. Then the Lord said in His heart, "I will never again curse the ground for man's sake, although the imagination of man's heart is evil from his youth; nor will I again destroy every living thing as I have done. (Genesis 8:20-21)

God transitioned Noah from the ark season to the altar season. You see, the ark season was about God *preserving life* through Noah. The altar season was about God *re-populating the world* through Noah. The ark season was about Noah's family while the altar season was about God's family. In this altar season, Noah was to take everything God had shown him in the boat through the storm and pass it on to somebody else.

You are to fill the hearts of people with the witness that if they will build what God tells them to build, they can survive any storm.

Somebody needs to know what you learned in your storm: what God showed you while you were in your storm fighting for your life. Somebody needs to know what you learned while you were going through the storm in your family, finances, health, and marriage. They need to learn what you learned. God didn't preserve you just for you—He preserved you so you would come out and fill your community, town, your small group, or your kids' ball team with the knowledge of the glory of the Lord. You are to fill the hearts of people with the witness that if you build what God tells you to build, you can survive any storm.

God has brought you through some storms, not just because He loves you, but because somewhere down the line, there will be someone else going through the same storm and they'll need to hear your story. They'll need to know how God brought you through. They'll need a living flesh example that says, "You know what? If I'm just faithful, if I just build the life He is telling me to build—if I'll build my business the way He's telling me to build it and if I'll build my family and my marriage on the rock, the way He's telling me to build them—the storms may come, but I'll survive *any* storm." They'll need *you* to give them a living, biblical example of what happened when you obeyed God.

Transitioning from Season to Season

You may be in that uncomfortable transitory period of your life where you've been faithful to build what God has called you to build for a season and now you're hearing the voice of God tell you to leave it behind. It isn't exactly fun when life demands that you move into the next season. You don't know how, you don't want to, and you wonder how to transition from the ark season to the altar season. When a certain job is all you've known, and you've built the "boat" of your job very well, and you've invested many years into building it—and now God is telling you to leave that boat behind—what do you do? How can you transition from this season into the next season?

There are three directions you need to look for help when it's time to move into your next season: look up, look forward, and look back.

Look up. When you're moving into the next season of your life, you need to look up. You need to continue your dialogue with the Lord. That's *dialogue*, not monologue. Monologue is just you talking. Dialogue is when you talk, and then you stop and listen for God's input. Powerful prayer is when you listen more than you talk. That means you need to operate in faith during your prayer time—believing God actually has something to speak to you. The things God has to say to you are much more important to your life than the things you have to say to God. Your conversation with God isn't just you going through your latest list of rants, complaints, problems, and issues of life. You need to also listen and let God speak to you—to reveal His plan for the next phase of your life.

We can't get so focused on life's circumstances that we can't stop and listen to God. There are going to be some things we'll come up against that we've never seen before. There are going to be plenty of opportunities to be afraid and doubt and feel full of anxiety; but if we continue to talk to God, and continue to *look up* to Him, He will order our steps.

> *I will lift up my eyes to the hills—*
> *From whence comes my help?*
> *My help comes from the Lord,*
> *Who made heaven and earth.* (Psalm 121:1-2)

Look up—not down. Stop looking at your circumstances or looking at yourself and asking if you can do what God is asking you to do. Just *look up* and say, "God, I can't do this without you." Talk to Him, and then take the time to stop and listen. He'll give you the direction, the wisdom, and the people you need to do everything He's called you to do. God isn't going to call you to something but fail to equip you for it. *Look up*—the answer is always there.

If we continue to talk to God, and continue to *look up* to Him, He will order our steps.

Look forward. Just as Noah had to look forward past the storm to be fruitful, multiply, and affect untold generations of people, you and I have to look beyond ourselves as we move from one season to the next. Selfishness often manifests when it's time for us to look forward. We say, "I don't want to, God, this doesn't feel good. I'm not comfortable." We find ourselves saying "I" a whole lot in our monologues with God.

In fact, the expression of uncrucified will is telling God what "I want"; while the expression of a crucified will is asking God what He wants. The uncrucified soul says, "here's what I want, I think, and I feel." The crucified soul asks, "what does God think, God want, and God feel?"

When we're standing in the doorway of the ark and it's all we've ever known—it's all we're familiar with and all we're comfortable in—we find it hard when God asks us to move forward into the next season of our lives. Like Noah, God is telling you, "Come on, I'm calling you to a new season." You've never been there before, and you don't know what it's like. When God calls you to a new season and tells you it's time to leave that boat behind, you may find yourself stuck in selfishness. You have to look beyond your feelings and desires and look to another generation that God is calling us to affect. You have to *look forward* and take that step out of the ark.

God asks us to lay down our personal preferences and give up our opinions and comfort to look beyond ourselves to impact others.

Many of us say we'll do anything for the Lord. But, what most people really mean is that they'll do anything except lay down their personal preferences and give up their opinions and comfort. But God is telling us to look forward and look beyond ourselves. When you do that, you'll see there's a generation of people that your life, your calling, and your ministry will impact. But, first, you have to leave the boat.

People often want to begin the new season they're stepping into while they stay in the doorway of the boat. They want to look out to what God is calling them to do, but they try to do it from inside the boat they spent so long building. But here's the thing: you can't have your next season until you leave your old season completely behind. You have to fully move out of the ark.

God is a seasonal God and He moves us through

times and seasons.

Look back, but don't focus on what's behind you. Look behind you to see two specific things. First, look back to see that God has always been leading you from season to season. If you do this, you'll see that God has never orchestrated something in your life, told you to get to a place, and then told you just to stay there. God does not inhabit that which does not change. He is a God of growth. You'll see that He led you through one season to take you to the next season and then the next. He has always been leading you through the seasons in your life. It makes no difference how long this season has been. God is a seasonal god and He moves us through times and seasons. Some of our seasons last longer than others—like when you're in the season of raising your children or completing school. The secret is to watch for your current season to end and be willing to move forward into the next season when it's time.

Second, look back to see God has always been faithful. With every season of change, He has been right there with you. In every transition, He's required you to go through, He's been there. Each time you've moved into a new season, God has provided, protected, and brought things to you that you've never known before.

You may be scared to leave your boat of familiarity behind and step from this season to the next; nonetheless, just *look back* and see where God has brought you from and how far you've come. Realize that He has been faithful to provide, guide, and protect you. David expressed it beautifully in Psalm 37:25.

Once I was young, and now I am old. Yet I have never seen the godly abandoned or their children begging for bread (NLT).

God has been with you and He will continue to be with you. He's there when He calls you to build the boat, when He calls you to be in the boat, and when He calls you to leave the boat.

Leaving the Boat Key Points

• We need to let our lives demonstrate that we believe God's Word.

• We have to break the pattern of sending the raven before the dove.

• We need to live under the direction and power of the Holy Spirit.

• No matter your age, your past experience or how long you've been serving God, as long as there is breath in your body, God has a next season for you to move into.

• We can't focus on our investment and, in so doing, forfeit God's next season for our lives.

• You are to fill the hearts of people with the witness that if they will build what God tells them to build, they can survive any storm.

• If we continue to talk to God, and continue to look up to Him, He will order our steps.

• God asks us to lay down our personal preferences and give up our opinions and comfort to look beyond ourselves to impact others.

• God is a seasonal god and He moves us through times and seasons.

Leaving the Boat Action Steps

Read these suggested action steps and check them off as you complete them. Add your own as the Lord continues to instruct you.

* If you really believe the Word of God, then you're going to take a step of faith in response to what God has said. Does your life demonstrate that you believe in the promises of God? What is that step of faith you need to take? Take that step of faith today.

* Are you still trying to do it all by yourself? Call upon the Holy Spirit starting today and ask Him to guide you through your storm.

* Have you been looking at what you've invested in building, instead of being willing to move into your next season with God? Turn your face toward God and tell Him you're ready to move into your next season and leave what you have built behind.

* Stop looking at your circumstances or looking at yourself and asking if you can do this. Just look up and say, "God, I can't do this without you."

* Look behind you. Do you see how God has led you through various seasons of your life? List those seasons. Then go back and describe how God has been faithful to provide everything you needed in each of those seasons.

* Take the time to write up your testimony and be prepared to give it when God gives you the opportunity. You should be able to give your testimony in five minutes. By writing it out and practicing it, you will be ready when God calls you to share it.

* There's somebody in your life right now who needs to know what you went through in this long, dark journey, just to come out on the other side and say I am here to tell you God is faithful. What's that person's name? Be obedient and go share your testimony with him or her.

Chapter 6

The Other Side of the Storm

And Noah began to be a farmer, and he planted a vineyard. Then he drank of the wine and was drunk, and became uncovered in his tent. And Ham, the father of Canaan, saw the nakedness of his father, and told his two brothers outside. But Shem and Japheth took a garment, laid it on both their shoulders, and went backward and covered the nakedness of their father. Their faces were turned away, and they did not see their father's nakedness. So Noah awoke from his wine, and knew what his younger son had done to him. Then he said: "Cursed be Canaan; a servant of servants He shall be to his brethren." And he said: Blessed be the Lord, The God of Shem, and may Canaan be his servant. May God enlarge Japheth, and may he dwell in the tents of Shem; and may Canaan be his servant." And Noah lived after the flood three hundred and fifty years. So all the days of Noah were nine hundred and fifty years; and he died. (Genesis 9:20-28)

This marked a major transition in Noah's life. Noah had walked with God, listened to God's voice, and obeyed Him. Then, we read that Noah got drunk, got naked, cursed his son, and died. As I read this I am thinking, "Really? This can't be the last thing said about Noah."

In the first three chapters about Noah's life, Noah is so close to God—and has such an intimate walk with God—that you think that Noah has it all together. You think Noah has it all figured out. In fact, the King James Version uses the word "perfect" in describing Noah. You'd think this is a guy who is walking the walk.

In fact, we get this impression that not only is Noah walking the walk, but so is his family. We think they're a picture-perfect family with no dysfunction. You wouldn't find them on Jerry Springer! You may even think, "They're such a great family, I just can't relate to them. My family is a far-cry from that." Think about it. This is a family who worked side-by-side building the ark for about seventy-five years and then spent thirteen months confined inside. Noah is with his wife, three adult sons, their wives, a bunch of animals, and all their *mess*. Your family can't even get through Disney World with your kids without almost committing murder and here's a guy who stayed locked up in the same boat with all of his family for thirteen months.

The Bible doesn't tell us how long the gap is between when Noah left the ark and when he got drunk and naked in his tent. But, it had to be at least long enough to grow a grape vineyard that would yield enough fruit to make juice. Since one does not get drunk from grape juice, the juice also had to have time to ferment into wine. So, this event didn't happen a day, week, month or even a year after Noah left the ark.

However long it took, we get down to the end of chapter nine and realize that Noah *was not* perfect. The only perfect person who ever walked the earth was Jesus. Noah was just a normal, average guy. This seemingly perfect man had an imperfect moment in his life, and it affected a lot of people. This raises the question: "Was this something that was in Noah's heart all along or was this just a solitary stumble in Noah's life?"

Noah was not perfect. He was just a normal, average guy.

The Bible doesn't give us many details about that moment in Noah's life, but here's what we do know: Noah's actions didn't take God by surprise. God knew it was going to happen all along, yet, He chose Noah anyway. God wasn't having a moment where He was scratching His head as Noah was having this time of stupidity in the tent. God wasn't saying, "Man, I didn't see that one coming. Noah really surprised me." He wasn't saying, "If I had known that Noah had the capacity to do this, I wouldn't have chosen him in the first place."

Noah engaged in one of the very activities that God had just purged from the earth; but God didn't say, "I wish I'd never called Noah. I didn't know *that* was going to happen." God knew the potential of Noah engaging in this act of naked drunkenness—because God understood Noah's end from his beginning. The volume of Noah's days was written in God's book, just like yours are. God realized that Noah was going to mess up, yet, He called and chose him *anyway*. God used an imperfect person to bring about redemption in his generation.

God can use an imperfect person like you to impact your generation and change the world.

Noah was just a messed up, normal, average person who was flawed and could give way to the flesh and sin. Noah had good days and bad days, good seasons and bad seasons, and obedient times and disobedient times. But God used Noah anyway. The best part is this: God didn't just use people like Noah *then*—He still uses people like Noah *now*. When you realize that, then you understand that if God can use a messed-up person like Noah, he can use a messed-up person like you.

But as the days of Noah were, so also will the coming of the Son of Man be. For as in the days before the flood, they were eating and drinking, marrying and giving in marriage, until the day that Noah entered the ark, and did not know until the flood came and took them all away, so also will the coming of the Son of Man be. (Matthew 24:37-39)

It was dark, messed up, and perverse in Noah's day. You may not realize it, but it's pretty dark, and messed up, and perverse in our day. In 2016 there were over 44,000 suicides just in the United States—and that rate continues to climb each year. In fact, there are more people right now who enter eternity by taking their own lives than by vehicle accidents. There are 1.2 million abortions in the United States each year. There are about a million divorces every year in this nation. Perhaps the most alarming statistic to highlight how dark and perverse our generation is this: almost $3,100 dollars are spent on the pornographic industry *every second.*

So, what's that saying? Simply that if God can use an imperfect man like Noah to affect his generation; then God can use an imperfect person like you to impact your generation and change the world.

Here's what I want you to understand right now: God chose and used Noah in a great, significant, and lasting way. Noah survived the storm and came through to the other side. He built what God called him to build, and God used him in a powerful way. Noah's family was saved and would bring about God's plan in the new season of their lives.

> *These three were the sons of Noah, and from these the whole earth was populated.* (Genesis 9:19)

Think about this: Noah's family was dominating the world. Nothing was happening or being built or taking place in the earth that couldn't be connected and traced back to Noah and his family. In our time, we'd call Noah a pretty successful man with a pretty successful family. They were what we would call "world changers." Today, we would think about certain family dynasties like the Kennedys, Rockefellers, or Rothschilds who seemed to be touching and affecting every aspect of society. In Noah's day, that was *his* family. Everything was connected to them.

When Noah got to the other side of the storm, he let his guard down.

The Other Side of the Storm

Here's what I think happened: When Noah got to the other side of the storm, he let his guard down. He made it through the storm season, entered the altar season, and gave all the glory to God for surviving the storm. He obeyed God, walked away from the ark, and began his new season. He and his family had been through one exciting ride. They came through the flood and the storm, and left the safety of the ark to step into a whole new world—a world that now revolved around them.

It's the same for us. We come through our family storms, financial storms, marriage storms, and health crisis storms. We make it to the other side of our storm. Your life is still wet from the rains of the storm, and your testimony is, "Had it not been for the Lord who is on my side, my enemy would have swallowed me up."

We end up forgetting that the only reason we made it through was because of God's goodness and God's grace.

But once you get a little distance between yourself and the storm that God brought you through, it's very easy to merge together God's grace with your intellect, talent, and hard work. When you do that, your testimony ends up transforming a little at a time—like the proverbial "fish tale." What used to be, "I only made it through by the grace of God" morphs into, "Well, you know, I'm a really hard worker. I spent years building this amazing ark, and it was so well built that it survived the biggest storm in history." Your testimony ends up changing from, "God had His hand upon me, God spared me, and God spoke to me," to, "Well, you know, I had a really good idea, and I'm just really talented, and I'm well-connected, and look what I did. It changed the world!"

What happened? You forgot that the only reason you made it through was because of God's goodness and grace. You forgot that the only reason you built the ark and it survived the storm is because God gave you the design for the ark in the first place. You forgot the only reason that your family made it through was because of God's provision.

On the other side of the storm and the flood, Noah let his guard down and pride began to enter in. He came to a point of destruction in his life. How can I say that Noah became prideful? The Bible gives me that truth.

Pride goes before destruction, and a haughty spirit before a fall.
(Proverbs 16:18)

The Stink of Pride

Anywhere there is destruction—whether it's in a person, a family, or a nation—it comes only after pride has reared its ugly head. The problem is that so many of us don't realize that we're dealing with pride in our lives until we come to the point of destruction. Below the surface, there's a seed of pride that started to grow. God has been warning you and letting you know you need to search your heart and crucify that pride. God knows you need to deal with the pride before destruction sets in. However, many of us refuse to acknowledge the warning signs God has been sending us. It's particularly hard for us to see those warning signs right after we've survived a great storm.

It's just like driving down the road on your way to a great vacation after you've worked particularly hard and made it through a rough patch in your life. You're sailing along, looking forward to the wonderful vacation God has sent you on, when you see a warning sign that the bridge has washed out on the road ahead of you. You know you *deserve* this vacation, so you ignore the warning signs. You think you're so deserving that the signs of imminent danger somehow don't apply to you. Besides, the route you're on is the quickest way to get where you're going. You figure there will be another exit off the highway, and this will not be a problem for you. After all, this is much smaller than the storm that you just weathered. So, there you are: driving down the road surrounded by signs that the bridge ahead of you is out. But you choose to ignore them all.

If we responded to the signs on the road like we sometimes respond to God, we would be getting offended as the number and frequency of the signs increased. "How dare the highway department put those signs in front of me? I'm just enjoying my drive. Don't they know that those signs are offensive to me? What right do they have to tell me how to drive? They can't tell me what to do! They don't know me." But if we keep going down that road, and we refuse to heed the warnings, we are going to come to a point of destruction.

If we are truly honest with ourselves, we would admit that is how we act with God sometimes. God is letting us know (through people in our lives, the Word, teaching, preaching, and various other means) that the road we're going down is a road called pride. And the road only leads one way: to destruction.

Anywhere there is destruction—whether it's in a person, a family, or a nation—it comes only after pride has reared its ugly head.

Pride is like body odor: You don't know you have it, but everybody around you knows you have it. God has some people in your life that He's put there to whom you need to listen as they try to tell you that you stink a little bit. They try to tell you there is the smell of pride wafting off you. Nobody wants to be around you when you stink. You have to really love somebody to put up with a nasty stink of body odor, and it's the same with the stink of pride.

A good friend is one who pulls you aside and says, "Hey, you might want to think of changing your brand of deodorant. It doesn't seem to be working. You're giving off an offensive odor." Just like good friends, God has people He'll put in your life who are there to let you know your pride stinks. They are there to warn you that if you don't deal with it, you're headed for destruction.

That's where Noah was. He had a great track-record up to this point, but he let his guard down. We all have the potential to let pride get the best of us, especially after an amazing victory in our lives. We get to the other side of the flood, we get on the other side of the storm that God has brought us through, and we slowly begin to forget that God was the only way we made it to the other side.

When you have eaten and are full, then you shall bless the Lord your God for the good land which He has given you. "Beware that you do not forget the Lord your God by not keeping His commandments, His judgments, and His statutes which I command you today, lest—when you have eaten and are full, and have built beautiful houses and dwell in them; and when your herds and your flocks multiply, and your silver and your gold are multiplied, and all that you have is multiplied; when your heart is lifted up, and you forget the Lord your God who brought you out of the land of Egypt, from the house of bondage. (Deuteronomy 8:10-14)

We're not smart enough to have gone through that storm without God. No matter how many storms we survive, no matter how greatly God uses us and no matter what we build, we must not forget that the story will always be about God's grace—and never about our perfection. The theme of the story of your life is not you; rather, the theme is Jesus and the grace that He has demonstrated in your life.

You see, we've been studying Noah's ark and Noah's flood. You can see his folly. In Noah's flood, his family was spared, and the world was destroyed. In Noah's folly, his family was destroyed, and the world was spared. In Noah's flood, his family was not affected by the sins of other people. But in Noah's folly, his family was destroyed because of his sins.

We all have the capacity to make dumb decisions, to disobey God, to rebel against Him, and yet, in all of that, God chooses us.

The Expiration Date

What really happened here? Noah's perfection ran out. His ability to live a perfect life had an expiration date.

The milk in your refrigerator has an expiration date—a date after which it will no longer be "good" for consumption. Noah's goodness, his perfection, his ability to live a good and perfect life, also had an expiration date. Your ability in and of your flesh to be good, to be perfect, and to be holy has an expiration date. You can wake up tomorrow morning and say, "I'm going to be good today. I'm going to be holy today. I'm going to be perfect today. I'm going to cross every 't.' I'm going to dot every 'i.' And

I'm even going to dot each and every lower-case 'j' today. Today, I'm going to have it down." You may have a good hour, and possibly even a good day; but, ultimately, your goodness and your perfection will run out. It will reach its expiration date.

For many of us, we're good until somebody cuts us off in traffic on the way to work. Or maybe we're good until we're stuck in traffic, or until somebody takes our parking spot at the grocery store. Then, you "flash the bird" and show that parking-spot bandit how well-manicured the nail on your middle finger is. Our goodness and holiness have an expiration date. Take me for example. I can be the picture of holiness for about eight hours—and then I wake up and it is all downhill from there. Just like that, Noah's perfection ran out.

But we are all like an unclean thing, and all our righteousnesses are like filthy rags; we all fade as a leaf, and our iniquities, like the wind, have taken us away. (Isaiah 64:6)

The Scriptures reveal that our righteousness is as filthy rags. But here is the gospel, the good news: Jesus' goodness, holiness, and perfection do not have expiration dates.

Jesus Christ is the same yesterday, today, and forever. (Hebrews 13:8)

So, the secret we must learn from all of this is that our faith and our hope and our trust is not in *our* holiness, goodness, or righteousness. We must constantly renew our minds so that we are always prepared for the next calling, the next adventure. Our faith is in the fact that He was holy, He is holy, and He ever will be holy. In fact, He is so holy that the angels and the creatures in heaven cry out around Him, twenty-four hours a day, "holy, holy, holy is the Lord God Almighty which is, and was, and is to come." I don't put my faith in my ability to be good. I put my faith in the fact that He is always good, He is always righteous, He is always holy. And I am in Him.

For I am not ashamed of the gospel of Christ, for it is the power of

*God to salvation for everyone who believes, for the Jew first and
also for the Greek. For in it the righteousness of God is revealed
from faith to faith; as it is written, "The just shall live by faith."*
(Romans 1:16-17)

Key Points

• God can use an imperfect person like you to impact your
generation and change the world.

• When Noah got to the other side of the storm, he let his guard
down.

• We end up forgetting that the only reason we made it through
was because of God's goodness and God's grace.

• Anywhere there is destruction—whether it's in a person, a
family, or a nation—it comes only after pride has reared its ugly
head.

• We all have the capacity to make dumb decisions, to disobey
God, to rebel against Him, and yet, in all of that, God chooses
us.

Action Steps

Read these suggested action steps and check them off as
you complete them. Add your own as the Lord continues to
instruct you.

* We all have the potential to have pride get the best of
us—especially after an amazing victory in our lives. We get to
the other side of the flood, we get on the other side of the storm
that God has brought us through, and we slowly begin to forget
that the only way we got through it was God. Have you had this
experience? How could you use your experience to help others
not succumb to pride after they make it through their storm?

* We all have the capacity to make dumb decisions, to disobey
God, to rebel against Him, and yet in all of that God chooses us.
When was the last time you did one of these imperfect things?
What was the outcome? What did you learn about yourself?
What did you learn about God?

* So, the secret you must learn from all of this is that your faith, hope, and trust is not in your holiness, or your goodness, or your righteousness. Put your faith in Jesus, because He is always good, He always righteous, He is always holy, and you are in Him.

Final Word

Be Encouraged!

Here's what I'm not saying: I'm not saying that you're going to mess up, so there's no reason to try. Not at all. Here's what I *am* telling you: God *knew* Noah was going to mess up and have a dumb moment—and He chose Noah anyway. And just like God knew that truth about Noah, God knows the same thing about you. He knows you're going to mess up and have some dumb moments. *And He chooses you anyway.* God knows you may have a good span of six months, then you're going to get distracted. He knows you'll have a bad span of two or three months, and then you're going to come back. God knew you were going to be raised in the church until you were eighteen, and that the day you turned eighteen, you were going to walk away and say, "this isn't for me." He knew you were going to live for yourself until you were about forty, and then when all hell broke loose, you'd say, "I need to come back to God." God knew that before any of it happened. God knew that you would spend a season of your life in church on Sunday but live like the devil the other six days of the week. He knew that. God knows all about you, and yet, He calls you anyway. He chooses you anyway.

God's Perfect Knowledge of Man

O LORD, You have searched me and known me.

You know my sitting down and my rising up;

You understand my thought afar off.

You comprehend my path and my lying down,

And are acquainted with all my ways.

For there is not a word on my tongue,

But behold, O LORD, You know it altogether.

You have hedged me behind and before,

And laid Your hand upon me.

Such knowledge is too wonderful for me;

It is high, I cannot attain it.

Where can I go from Your Spirit?

Or where can I flee from Your presence?

If I ascend into heaven, You are there;

If I make my bed in hell, behold, You are there.

If I take the wings of the morning,

And dwell in the uttermost parts of the sea,

Even there Your hand shall lead me,

And Your right hand shall hold me.

If I say, "Surely the darkness shall fall on me,"

Even the night shall be light about me;

Indeed, the darkness shall not hide from You,

But the night shines as the day;

The darkness and the light are both alike to You.

For You formed my inward parts;

You covered me in my mother's womb.

I will praise You, for I am fearfully and wonderfully made;

Marvelous are Your works,

And that my soul knows very well.

My frame was not hidden from You,

When I was made in secret,

And skillfully wrought in the lowest parts of the earth.

Your eyes saw my substance, being yet unformed.

And in Your book they all were written,

The days fashioned for me,

When as yet there were none of them. (Psalm 139:1-16)

God is acquainted with all of your ways; not just your good ones—not just your Sunday school ones. Noah's failure didn't take God by surprise, and your failure doesn't take God by surprise either. Just like God was acquainted with Noah's ways, He is acquainted with *your* ways.

I've come to realize I'm not even acquainted with all my ways. Did you ever have a time when you responded to something in a way that surprised you, and you said, where did that come from? You say, "I didn't know I would do that. I didn't know I would think like that or react that way. I didn't see that one coming." That happened to me recently and it made me realize I'm not acquainted with all of my ways.

I was sitting in my chair on a Saturday afternoon, starting to get ready for Sunday's service. I laid back in my recliner, trying to clear my mind, and began to slip into a good Holy-Ghost-filled nap. Ten minutes is all I need for a good power nap. My wife came into the room and thought she'd be funny. She quietly came over next to me while I wasn't totally out. I was in between—in that state of almost asleep, but not quite. I was just conscious enough to tell that somebody was hovering over the top of me. I felt somebody right over me, kind of like a "disturbance in the force." I barely opened my eyes and saw somebody or something right above my face.

I think my first thought was somebody had broken into the house, and was about to kill me, or strangle me or something. My initial reaction was to throw up a fist. It wasn't a conscious decision. It was just a reaction. All of a sudden, fight or flight just kicked in. I jerked up and raised up my fist, and I smacked my wife. I am now a wife beater. I hit my wife right square in the face.

Now, before you throw this book in the trash, I didn't break her nose or anything like that. We didn't end up taking a trip to the ER. I didn't have to pick her up off the floor. I barely made contact. In fact, she thought it was hilarious. She was laughing so hard, I thought she would fall over. Still, I felt awful. The whole point is that when I realized what I had done, I wondered, "Where'd that come from? I'm not a ninja. I'm not one of those guys who sleeps with one eye open, always thinking someone is coming after me. What in the world possessed me to respond that way?" I didn't know I would respond like that. I wasn't acquainted with all of my ways.

There are times in your life when you're going to say, "Where did that come from? I didn't know that I thought that way, or that I would respond that way." We don't even know our own ways, but God does. He knows all of the messed up, faulty ways buried deep within us—yet He chooses us anyway. We all have some twisted, crooked ways that need to be straightened out. But, yet, God chooses us to build and do His work anyway. God says, "I'm calling you. I'm choosing you. Don't think you have to fix all your ways before I can choose you. *I'll* fix your ways. Don't think you have to get all of your crooked places straight before I can use you. *I'll* straighten them out. I'll take care of them. Just know that I am calling you."

> *Remember, dear brothers and sisters, that few of you were wise in the world's eyes or powerful or wealthy when God called you. Instead, God chose things the world considers foolish in order to shame those who think they are wise. And he chose things that are powerless to shame those who are powerful.* **God chose things despised by the world, things counted as nothing at all, and used them to bring to nothing what the world considers important. As a result, no one can ever boast in the presence of God.** *God has united you with Christ Jesus. For our benefit God made him to be wisdom itself. Christ made us right with God; he made us pure and holy, and he freed us from sin. Therefore, as the Scriptures say, "If you want to boast, boast only about the LORD."* (I Corinthians 1:26-31

NLT emphasis added)

Perfection is not a prerequisite for being used by God. God may have a great call that He is speaking to you about. He has been trying to pull you out of the status quo and telling you it's really time to get intentional. He's been trying to tell you it's time to really get focused. We use lots of excuses as to why we can't do what we *know* God is calling us to do. We tell ourselves what's wrong with the plan, the timing, and the logistics. We look at what isn't where we think it needs to be in our lives. But, God is calling us in spite of all of that.

Perfection is not a prerequisite for being used by God.

God says He chooses the unwise, the non-influential, the foolish, the weak, the lowly, and the despised. God chooses those who are considered nothing by the world's standards. But know this: whatever you've been told you are not, God chooses you and says *you are*. Whatever you think you're not capable of doing, if God chooses you and calls you, then you can do it. Every single one of us has gone through a time in our journey of life when people told us we're not wise, or we're not good enough, or we are not powerful enough. We've had circumstances tell us we can't do this thing. We look at our lives and think we're nothing, we're not smart enough, holy enough, religious enough, or old enough. We don't have enough money or enough connections to build what God is calling us to build.

We've let it build up and build up, as we go through life to the point that when we get the call, all we can say is, "I am not. I cannot." It becomes an excuse that we hide behind to not build the life God calls us to build. We say we can't build the marriage or the family, or the career, or that business God has called us to build. We hide behind all of these things that we say we are not. We disqualify ourselves. We un-call ourselves because somebody told us we "are not" and we agreed with them. We believed the lie. Yet, here is what the Word of God says: "God calls those who are not."

God says He chooses the unwise, the non-influential, the foolish, the weak, the lowly, and the despised.

So, you say you aren't smart enough? God called you. You don't like the calling? God called you. You say you aren't religious enough? God called you. You say you don't have enough or you aren't enough of this or that? God called you. I want to challenge and provoke you and tell you that you don't have another excuse. Your excuses are gone. It's time to get busy. It's time to start building what God has called you to build. The excuses that you've been hiding behind are over. God calls those who are not. It doesn't matter anymore what others have told you that you are not. It no longer matters what you told yourself you are not. If God has called you, then He says *you are and you can.* Obedience is our only path. He tells you why you can do it, too: "God has united you with Christ Jesus."

God wants to set you free from what you believed you are not. Some things that have defined you and limited you, God is saying it's time to move beyond, and rise above them, and let this be your uprising moment. Perhaps you've let the limitations of what people have said—and maybe even the things you've said yourself—hold you down and hold you back from building the life God wants you to build. The future is ready, and God is calling you to build. Don't allow your thoughts about what you "are not" to hold you back. Realize God has chosen you. If God is for you, what storm can come against you? It's time to rise up and build and be active about your Father's business. God says you can survive any storm and accomplish what He has called you to do. Get to work.

And we know that God causes everything to work together for the good of those who love God and are called according to his purpose for them. For God knew his people in advance, and he chose them to become like his Son, so that his Son would be the firstborn among many brothers and sisters. And having chosen them, he called them to come to him. And having called them, he gave them right standing with himself. And having given them right standing, he gave them his glory. What shall we say about such wonderful things as these? **If God is for us, who can ever be against us?** *Since he did not spare even his own Son but gave him up for us all, won't he also give us everything else?* (Romans 8:28-32 NLT emphasis added)

Day 1

When you look around you today, do you get the feeling that things have to change? What has to change?

_____

_____

_____

_____

_____

_____

_____

_____

_____

_____

_____

Day 2

What darkness do you see around you?

_____

_____

_____

_____

_____

_____

_____

_____

_____

_____

_____

_____

Day 3

Remember, God's wrath poured out over people's thoughts, not actions. What is your thought life like? What do you meditate on daily?

_____

_____

_____

_____

_____

_____

_____

_____

_____

_____

_____

Day 4

Write down 3 scriptures that you can commit to memory to align your thoughts with God's:

_____

_____

_____

_____

_____

_____

_____

_____

_____

_____

_____

_____

_____

_____

Day 5

Noah had no support system. No resources. What support system and resources do you have to aid you in being a light in the darkness?

_____

_____

_____

_____

_____

_____

_____

_____

_____

_____

_____

_____

Day 6

Everyone around Noah lived for the moment, but he lived for the legacy. Are you contributing to your legacy? What do you want your legacy to be?

_____

_____

_____

_____

_____

_____

_____

_____

_____

_____

_____

Day 7

Is there ever a time in your life where you felt God calling you to build something or do something and you ignored Him because it felt too hard, impossible, or inconvenient? What was that like?

_____

_____

_____

_____

_____

_____

_____

_____

_____

_____

_____

Day 8

What is God calling you to build now?

_____

_____

_____

_____

_____

_____

_____

_____

_____

_____

_____

_____

_____

_____

Day 9

What skills do you need for your calling? Who do you need in your life for your calling?

_____

_____

_____

_____

_____

_____

_____

_____

_____

_____

_____

_____

Day 10

What is holding you back? Is it your past, your knowledge, your level of hope, etc.?

_____

_____

_____

_____

_____

_____

_____

_____

_____

_____

_____

_____

_____

Day 11

Can you think of a time in your life when you were assigned a project at work you didn't feel qualified for or God asked you to do something you didn't feel ready for? Was there a time in your life where you had to move on to another life stage before you felt ready? What did that feel like? What was the outcome?

_____

_____

_____

_____

_____

_____

_____

_____

_____

_____

_____

Day 12

God is more concerned about your daily walk than your calling, because you can't have one without the other. What does your daily walk with God look like, and how can you improve it?

_____

_____

_____

_____

_____

_____

_____

_____

_____

_____

_____

_____

Day 13

Think of the times in your life where you KNOW that you heard from God. What was that like? How do you usually hear from God?

_____

_____

_____

_____

_____

_____

_____

_____

_____

_____

_____

_____

Day 14

Are you ready to put in the work to build your ark? Are you healthy mentally, physically, spiritually, emotionally, and intellectually? List one way in each of those areas that you can improve your overall "health."

Mental

Physical

Spiritual

Emotional

Intellectual

_____

_____

_____

_____

_____

_____

_____

_____

_____

Day 15

Now that you've described your calling, what is your *vision*? Write down your vision for your personal life, work life, and calling.

_____

_____

_____

_____

_____

_____

_____

_____

_____

_____

_____

_____

Day 16

If you don't have a vision, everyone around you will have a vision for you. Who are you letting speak into your life?

_____

_____

_____

_____

_____

_____

_____

_____

_____

_____

_____

_____

Day 17

Who should you be letting speak into your life? Make a list of people who are successful in your arena i.e. successful at raising a family, successful at your industry, successful in their walk with God, etc... Contact them for coffee or fellowship. Ask them questions.

_____

_____

_____

_____

_____

_____

_____

_____

_____

_____

_____

Day 18

How is your focus? Do you flit from project to project, leaving things undone? What can you do to focus better?

_____

_____

_____

_____

_____

_____

_____

_____

_____

_____

_____

_____

_____

Day 19

Can you think of a time when you had a calling or a task that you abandoned? What was the outcome? What would've been the outcome if you had stuck with it to completion?

_____

_____

_____

_____

_____

_____

_____

_____

_____

_____

_____

Day 20

Think of a time when you blamed someone in the past for a mistake or error. Think of a time when you were blamed for something that may or may not have been your fault. How did that feel? How did they/you react? Was it worth it?

_____

_____

_____

_____

_____

_____

_____

_____

_____

_____

_____

_____

Day 21

Is there a time when you felt like you tried to "modify" God's design? You tried to complete God's calling with your own blueprints? How did that work out?

_____

_____

_____

_____

_____

_____

_____

_____

_____

_____

_____

_____

Day 22

Are there preparation steps you feel like God is nudging you toward? What can you do to be better prepared for the storm coming. Is it education, repentance, relationships, etc . . . ?

_____

_____

_____

_____

_____

_____

_____

_____

_____

_____

_____

Day 23

Are you leading your life with a raven or a dove? Are you leading with your flesh or allowing the Holy Spirit to go before you?

_____

_____

_____

_____

_____

_____

_____

_____

_____

_____

_____

_____

Day 24

We can't focus on our investment into a storm and forget to get off the boat. Is there a time in your life when you dwelled a little too long in a season because you didn't want to let go? Describe it?

_____

_____

_____

_____

_____

_____

_____

_____

_____

_____

_____

_____

Day 25

Are you currently in a storm, leaving a storm, or entering a storm?
What do you think your next season will be? Dream about it
below.

_____

_____

_____

_____

_____

_____

_____

_____

_____

_____

_____

_____

_____

Day 26

When you finish a storm, do you write down what you learned?
Write down things you've learned in difficult storms in your life.
How can you use that to help others going through the same thing?

_____

_____

_____

_____

_____

_____

_____

_____

_____

_____

_____

Day 27

How do your personal opinions and preferences hold you back from influencing others?

_____

_____

_____

_____

_____

_____

_____

_____

_____

_____

_____

_____

Day 28

When you think about those storms in your life, do you truly remember that it was God who brought you through? Or have you begun to rationalize your own abilities and role?

_____

_____

_____

_____

_____

_____

_____

_____

_____

_____

_____

_____

Day 29

Can you think of a moment when your pride got in your way?
What was the outcome? Did you lose relationships or resources?
Did you forget to point to God? What would it have been like
otherwise?

_____

_____

_____

_____

_____

_____

_____

_____

_____

_____

_____

_____

Day 30

God chooses us despite anything. Think of a time when God chose you despite your own decisions, character flaws, and mistakes. Write about it below,

_____

_____

_____

_____

_____

_____

_____

_____

_____

_____

_____

_____

Acknowledgments

Thank you to my family: my parents, Mike and Lisa, and my brother, Chris. I love you all deeply, and I truly appreciate your support.

Thank you to my editor, Lora Adkins. You and Duran are the embodiment of this message, if you build what God tells you to build, you can survive any storm.

Thank you to all the amazing staff and leaders of Connection Church. I'm privileged to serve alongside some of the greatest people in the world. It's an honor leading people to know and grow in Jesus with you. There's no one else I'd rather "build a boat to change the world" with than the folks in eastern Kentucky.

Richard Holmes

Photo Credit: Jami Tackett and Tyler Stanley

Made in the USA
Coppell, TX
02 December 2020

42678795R00073